# You Don't Have to Be Famous to Write a Memoir

Stephen Mark Silvers

Interior typesetting by Kerry Ellis

Cover design by Rafael Andres

Cover illustration by Isabella Newcomer (my granddaughter)

## DEDICATION
In memory of Neusa

Amor da minha vida, minha "Abelha Rainha"

# CONTENTS

# PROLOGUE

**It was a dreary, overcast, rainy Seattle afternoon** when I first began writing this memoir, and in fact, at the time, I didn't know I was going to write a memoir. I had no intention of writing one; the thought never occurred to me. It began as a single Facebook post (*My Roads Not Taken*) in which I told the story of how I (a future Spanish teacher) inexplicably chose to go to Portuguese-speaking Brazil instead of Spanish-speaking Peru, one of the happiest, most fortuitous, life-changing decisions of my life.

For me, the post was to be a "one-off" story. Well, that post received a lot of positive comments, which inspired me to tell another story, again without any thought of telling the story of my life. Once again, more encouragement, and then yet again another story. Finally, after a number of Facebook posts, I decided I would write my life story.

So, this is my story. Perhaps I should begin by saying, as Kurt Vonnegut (1922–2007) did in *Slaughterhouse-five:* "All this happened, more or less." That is, I have told my story to the best of my memory. The thing about memory is that sometimes we remember things that never happened and forget things that did. But I would say, all in all, my memoir is accurate. However, it's not based solely on my memory. The things I remembered were checked against personal and family documents. Also, this memoir was produced, like the Beatles song, *With a Little Help from My Friends* (without the information supplied by cousins,

I couldn't have produced the stories about my maternal and paternal grandparents).

While I did post all of my stories on Facebook as I wrote them, the real audience for my memoir is me. I wrote it for me. I wrote it because I wanted to reminisce and make a record of the people, places, and events in my life. But also, I wrote it for my kids and my grandchildren. Now they'll have a record of my life. There are so many things I would like to ask my parents and my grandparents, but when we're young, we don't, and when we're older, it's too late. This memoir is also for family and friends. Finally, it's for anyone who would like to read a (hopefully) fun story about a "boomer" who grew up (kind of) Jewish, was in the Boy Scouts, had typical college experiences, and wound up teaching English in Brazil for thirty-seven years.

There are a few aspects of my memoir I'd like to briefly comment on. You'll find lots of digressions in which a thought brings to my mind something that is somehow (often loosely) associated with it (like a word association game in which you have to say the first thought that comes to your mind). The digressions often present "fun facts" or "fun quotes."

Throughout the book you'll find mentions of famous (and not-so-famous) people, historic events, places, books, songs, movies, and even a few curious fads, etc. I'd like to think of these mentions as a "pointer" to someone or something you might want to learn more about. Most of them can be found in *Wikipedia*, my go-to site for general information. The songs and even some movies can be found on *YouTube.*

Sometimes I comment, "Freud can explain this" (or I just say, "Hello, Freud!). This is a common expression in Brazil. It isn't used in a scientific sense, as a scientific explanation, but rather as a (usually) comical comment on a situation. For example, if you forget a person's name, then you (or a friend) might jokingly say, "Freud can explain this."

I've organized the memoir around six distinct periods in my life:

- First memories: around 1954

- Youngstown, Ohio: 1954–1964

- California: 1964–1967

- California: 1967–1971

- Brazil: 1972–2010

- Seattle: 2010–present

Besides the Prologue and Finis, there are two sections that don't fall into specific time frames: Part One: All in the Family (about me, my siblings, my parents, and my grandparents), and Part Eight: A Few More Stories.

Finally, don't read this as you normally do when you read a book or a magazine article, but instead try to imagine that you're *listening* to me telling my stories on The Moth or that you're a psychoanalyst and I'm lying on your couch talking about my life. Just don't imagine I'm Alexander Portnoy from Philip Roth's 1969 novel, *Portnoy's Complaint.* Jacqueline Susann, author of *Valley of the Dolls*, famously said about Philip Roth, "He's a good writer, but I wouldn't want to shake hands with him." If you've read *Portnoy's Complaint,* you'll understand her comment.

So, now, Let's get this show on the road.

# PART ONE:

# ALL IN THE FAMILY

CHAPTER 1

# ME

**Call me Ishmael. No, that won't do. First of all**, it's not really my name. And secondly, it's plagiarism. I borrowed (OK, stole) it from Herman Melville (1819–1891). That's how he began *Moby-Dick,* and I thought if it worked so well for Melville (it's one of the most iconic first lines in literature), maybe it would be an auspicious (Look, I was an English teacher, so occasionally I'll throw in a more formal, impressive-sounding word) beginning for me.

I was born Stephen Mark Silverstein on December 22, 1947, in Los Angeles, California. According to the DNA ancestry service 23and Me, I'm 99.6 percent Ashkenazi Jewish (Jews of central or eastern European descent). I'm also 0.4 percent British/Irish. If I had known about my (piddling) British heritage, I would've taught my classes with a lordly British accent and used expressions like, "I just need to spend a penny" (use the toilet); "That's smashing" (fantastic); "I'm knackered (tired); "bloke" (guy); "mate" (friend); and "cheers" (good-bye).

I arrived (so to speak) at 2:13 a.m. So, I got off to an early start. They say, "The early bird gets the worm." But as Franklin D. Roosevelt (US president 1933–1945) remarked, "I think we consider too much the good luck of the early bird and not enough the bad luck of the early worm."

In 1951, my father changed our family name to "Silvers." The name "Silvers" brings to mind Phil Silvers (1911–1985), known for his role as Sargent Bilko on the 1957 TV show *You'll Never Get Rich*. Bilko is a fast-talking, conniving army officer who spends most of his time finagling others to do his work for him while he tries to wheedle money through harebrained, get-rich-quick schemes.

I'm a "boomer," a person born in the years following World War II. The name comes from the noun "boom," which means "rapid growth" (a boom in new office buildings). By extension, it refers to the time of skyrocketing birth rates following World War II. It was a time of great economic prosperity, and as a result, couples felt confident that they could comfortably support large families.

So, who am I? What am I like? What kind of things do I like? I'll try to answer those questions here. The rest of the book will be about family, friends, people, places, and events in my life.

I'm seventy-six years old (as I write this). Mark Twain (1835–1910) famously said, "Age is an issue of mind over matter. If you don't mind, it doesn't matter." And I don't mind. I try to maintain a positive attitude. As best as I can. I agree with George Burns (1896–1996): "You can't help getting older, but you don't have to get old." And he was true to his words. He was still doing stand-up comedy in Las Vegas at age ninety-seven!

My Uncle Norman once said, "Growing old isn't for sissies." True. It can have its challenges (but it has its rewards: I no longer have to worry if my socks match when I go out). And, as Larry Lorenzoni said, "Birthdays are good for you. Statistics show that the people who have the most live the longest."

I'm in reasonably good health. I couldn't run a marathon,

but then again, I wouldn't want to. I'm in fairly good shape for my age. But I can't hold a candle to Mick Jagger of the Rolling Stones, who at eighty still leaps and bounds around on the stage as if he were twenty years old and in an advertisement for Red Bull.

Briefly (because you will learn the specifics in later stories), I spent nearly forty happy years teaching English as a foreign language (EFL) in Brazil (1972–2010). I had a long and happy marriage. My wife, Neusa, was Brazilian (sadly she died in 2011). Our three children (Paula, Sérgio, and David) were born and raised in Brazil, and as young adults they moved to Seattle, where my sister was living.

I consider myself lucky. I live with my daughter and her family, and my two boys live nearby. My relationship with my kids couldn't be better. They always joke with me, tease me (no, I wasn't a pothead hippie). We're always together as a family, celebrating birthdays and other events or just getting together for a barbecue at my son Sérgio's house. My kids are caring, devoted, and thoughtful. They are always "there for me."

I have two beautiful granddaughters (Giovanna and Isabella, ages fifteen and nineteen) who are talented, studious, and respectful. (I know. A respectful teenager is an oxymoron, something contradictory, like a "cheerful pessimist." But it's true. They are respectful.) And now, two twin year-old grandsons (Leon and Raffael). I'm lucky to have the family I have.

Basically, I'm a happy person. Perhaps a better word is "content." Mine is a kind of quiet happiness. I'm a little reserved, not given to hilarity, loud, gleeful, animated merriment, or festivities (such as New Years or Carnival). I never roar with laughter. I'm more of a quiet chuckler. More of a spectator than a participant.

I'm a minimalist. I have few possessions. I don't keep things unless they're useful or sentimental. You would be surprised at how few articles of clothing I have. Makes it easier to decide what I'm going to wear. Imagine the problem former Philippine First Lady Imelda Marcos must have had in choosing what to wear for lunch. She had 3,000 pairs of shoes, 15 mink coats, 508 gowns, and 888 handbags.

I'm also somewhat of a worrier. A worrier, but not a "Chicken Little." You know, the little chicken that (after being struck on the head by an acorn while walking in the woods) went around telling everyone that "the sky is falling!"

My Zodiac sign is Capricorn, the goat. Capricorns are practical, pragmatic, prudent, careful, diligent, disciplined, patient, responsible, intellectual, reserved, pessimistic, miserly grudging, and can be stubborn.

I never took astrology and zodiac signs seriously. But to my surprise, basically, I agree, with some exceptions. I had an academic career, but I don't consider myself an "intellectual." It's true I'm pessimistic, but only about the future of humankind. I was going to say "mankind," but then I remembered my daughter and my granddaughter Isabella, who are both hard-core feminists.

I'm not miserly, but I spend within my means. I'm definitely not grudging. As to stubborn, I resolutely, staunchly, and firmly disagree, but my kids always (joke?) that I am, saying (in Portuguese) that I am "cabeça dura" (hard-headed).

And now some of my favorites:

- **POETS:** A. E. Housman; Edna St. Vincent Millay;

Robert Service;  William Wordsworth;  Felix Dennis.

- **POEMS:** Sea Fever;  Slow Dance;  Velvet Shoes;  Stop all the Clocks;  My Last Duchess;  The Superstitious Ghost;  The Flower-fed Buffaloes.

- **SHORT STORIES:** The Necklace;  Flight;  The Specter Bridegroom;  To Build a Fire;  The First Seven Years;  The Lady or the Tiger;  Dr. Heidegger's Experiment.

- **NOVELS/NOVELLAS:** Robinson Crusoe;  The Little Prince; Monsignor Quixote; The Remains of the Day.

- **NONFICTION AUTHORS:** George Burns;  Thomas Foster;  Jake Grogan;  A. J. Jacobs;  Eric Weiner; Bill Bryson; Sloane Crosley.

- **FICTION AUTHORS:** Thorne Smith;  Washington Irving; Truman Capote; Willa Cather; Milton Hatoum.

- **FILMS:** 50/50;  Love Actually;  St. Vincent;  To Sir with Love;  The Bucket List;  The Intouchables (French film).

- **SINGER/GROUPS:** Elton John;  Judy Collins;  Peter, Paul, and Mary;  Jack Jones;  Miriam Makeba.

- **SONGS:** Imagine;  Suzanne;  Both Sides Now;  The Windmills of your Mind;  Early Mornin' Rain;  Come Away with Me;  My Way;  You Don't Know Me (Caetano Veloso)

CHAPTER 2

# MY MOTHER

My mother was Rose Aron—Silverstein/Silvers—Van Holt—Hiles. She had three husbands (but not simultaneously): David Silverstein (my father), Bill Van Holt, and Darrel Hiles. She was born in 1921 and died in 2013 at the age of ninety-two.

In Hollywood, multiple marriages are common. Zsa Zsa Gabor (1917–2016), a Hungarian-American actress and socialite, was married nine times. She once commented, "I'm a marvelous housekeeper. Every time I leave a man, I keep his house." Elizabeth Taylor (1932–2011) was married eight times. But none of that compares to an American named Linda Wolf, who has been married an amazing twenty-three times. Her husbands have included a one-eyed convict, a homeless man, a Mormon preacher, a musician, and a plumber.

My mother and father were married on September 18, 1945, in Youngstown, Ohio. It was a double wedding. My mother was married in a joint ceremony with her sister, my Aunt Helen, who married Harold Chevlen.

So how did this come about? The year was 1945. My mother was twenty-four, living in Youngstown and had a boyfriend by the name of Murry. They broke up, and Mom was heartbroken. Her sister (my Aunt Mary) and my Uncle Bill were living in California. Aunt Mary invited my mom to come and spend time with them, for what my cousin Eric Chevlen termed "a geographical cure for her broken heart."

Aunt Helen and Uncle Harold, who had known each other since they were adolescents, were planning on getting married. Around this time, my mother met my dad through Aunt Mary and Uncle Bill. The story is that my mom called Aunt Helen to tell her about her new romantic interest (my dad) and suggested that they have a double wedding. So, not long after my mom and dad met, they were in Youngstown, getting married. How long? A surprisingly short time: only two weeks. Yes, my mom and dad were married after having known each other for only two weeks! (but, sadly, they divorced twenty-one years later).

Of course, not many couples act so quickly. Some couples are a little bit slower to "take the plunge." Take, for example, Octavio Guillen and Adriana Martinez of Mexico. They were engaged for sixty-seven years and were both eighty-two years old on their wedding day. Which reminds me of the poem *Too Have and Too Old* by Richard Armour (1906–1989):

> The bride, white of hair, is stooped over her cane
> Her faltering footsteps need guiding.
> While down the church aisle, with wan toothless smile,
> The groom in a wheelchair comes riding.
> And who is this elderly couple you ask?
> You'll find, when you've closely explored it,
> That here is that rare, most conservative pair,
> Who waited 'til they could afford it.

From an early age, my mother was a dancer. When they were around eleven, my mom and Aunt Helen were a dance team, performing tap dancing wearing costumes sewn by their mother (my grandmother), which she embellished with sequins and rhinestones. Later, as an adult, Mom danced professionally in night club acts under the stage name of Judy Lynn. My father also performed, playing the marimba. They didn't perform together as an act, but rather one came on after the other. They performed in cities and small towns near Youngstown.

Mom was also an actress, active in the local Youngstown Playhouse. She acted in *The Most Happy Fella; Death of a Salesman; Our Town;* and *Gypsy,* a musical loosely based on the memoirs of striptease artist Gypsy Rose Lee (1911–1970).

Mom's second husband was Bill Van Holt. They were married in 1970 and divorced in 1978. As I was no longer living at home, I didn't have much contact with Bill. He was a nice man and treated me, Maureen, and Jeff as though we were his natural kids and not his stepkids. Unfortunately, Bill had a drinking problem, which ultimately led to their divorce.

Mom eventually knew she had to leave the relationship. One day in January of 1977, when Bill was at work, Jeff and Maureen got Mom on a plane to Youngstown, where she stayed with Aunt Helen and Uncle Harold. Bill was upset that Mom had left him, but at the same time he understood. He was aware that his drinking had destroyed their relationship, and in fact, after their divorce, he expressed sorrow and remorse and apologized to Maureen. Bill was a good man, and I liked him.

After a few months in Youngstown, Mom moved to Cupertino, California, to be near her brother, my Uncle Norman. In August of 1977, Mom auditioned for and was chosen as the female lead in the play *The Mind with the Dirty Man,* a comedy about an X-rated filmmaker whose father is fighting for movie censorship. It was there that she met Darrell Hiles, who was working the lights for the show. In 1980, they were married. He was a nice man, and Mom and Darrell were happy together.

In September of 1984, late one evening, my phone rang (I was living in Brazil). It was my brother calling to tell me that Darrell had suffered a fatal heart attack. He was apparently in good health; he had never had any health problems. Darrell was only fifty-two when he died. They had been together for seven years.

Around 1999, Maureen noticed that Mom was having worrisome memory issues and arranged for her to be moved to an assisted-living facility in Seattle where she would be able to manage and watch over her care. Initially, Mom's mental decline wasn't pronounced. However, in 2003 she needed more care, and Maureen was able to get her into a nursing home, where she died in 2013. If there was an "outstanding daughter" award, then Maureen would receive it for the dedication and love she gave in managing Mom's care.

In closing, I want to remark on my mother's courage and sense of humor. She faced all of her difficulties (divorces, financial problems, death of a spouse) with a positive attitude, and, with the exception of Darrell's death, a sense of humor.

# CHAPTER 3

# MY FATHER

**My father was born in 1914 in Fort Dodge, Iowa,** and died in 1980 in Los Angeles, at the age of sixty-six. He was born David Silverstein, but in 1951 he changed his name (and the names of me, my brother, and sister) to Silvers. I don't know the reason for the change, but I believe it was because he was in show business, and a shorter name would be better for billing his act.

Dad played the marimba professionally in nightclubs, where he was billed as "fabulous David Silvers marimba virtuoso extraordinary." The marimba is played using mallets, a kind of long stick with a small round ball on the end. Dad modified the mallets, somehow making the balls light up so that when he played in the dark (two mallets in each hand!) the audience would only see a set of four fast-moving lit-up balls striking the marimba.

Dad certainly lived up to his billing as "extraordinary." His most spectacular number was Flight of the Bumblebee by Russian composer Rimsky-Korsakov (1844–1908). This fast-moving piece of music is challenging on the piano, and even more so on the marimba.

Dad was also a talented furniture maker (he made furniture for our house) and an artist. Around 1962, he took up oil painting. For us kids, me (age fourteen), Maureen (thirteen), and Jeff (eleven), it was embarrassing. We would have friends visiting us, and Dad would be painting or one of his paintings would be on display. What was so embarrassing? Dad painted nudes. To be clear, he did paintings of nudes; he didn't paint "in the nude." Around 1974, he began doing abstract paintings as well as Chinese watercolors.

Dad liked to cook. Me? Despite having earned a cooking merit badge in the Boy Scouts, I never liked to cook and have always avoided it as far as possible. To be truthful, I have no memory of having cooked when I lived in an apartment with roommates near UCLA. I must have because I didn't eat out in restaurants, but I have no memory of cooking (as we say in Brazil, Freud can explain this).

Once, when I was living in the graduate student dorm (1970), I went home with my dad on a Friday evening. (He worked at UCLA. More about that in a bit.) When we got to his apartment (he was divorced from my mom and lived in a one-bedroom apartment), we sat looking at each other, each of us silently waiting for the other to prepare dinner. Finally, Dad realized we were going to go to bed hungry and, with a smile, said, "I guess I'll make us something to eat."

During World War Two, Dad was a nurse's aide in Borneo, where he contracted a bad case of dysentery and was sent to recover in Australia. I remember he once told me that I had almost had an Australian mother. Just think, I could've been the star of the film Crocodile Dundee. Oh Well!

After the war, he met my mother, and in September of 1945 they were married in Youngstown, Ohio, in a double wedding ceremony jointly with my mother's sister, my Aunt Helen. In 1969, my father and mother separated and were later divorced

(1970).

Around 1973, Dad had a new person in his life, Millie, a widow who was a few years older than him. Dad had once again found happiness. They were soon living together. They took a cruise to the Caribbean, spent two weeks in Hawaii, and went to Las Vegas several times. In short, they had a good life together until Millie got sick and died (around 1978).

Sometimes we can look back and say that a certain event made all the difference in our lives. For me, my brother, and sister, that event was a decision that our dad made in 1964. We were living in Youngstown, Ohio. Dad decided that we were going to move to Los Angeles. He was having a hard time making ends meet, and also he hated the Youngstown winters—five months of freezing cold and deep snow—snow that was beautiful to see but awful to drive in (of course we kids didn't see it that way).

The move to Los Angeles resulted in me, my sister, and my brother first going to a community college and then completing our studies at major universities (me and Maureen at UCLA; Jeff at the University of California at Irvine). If we had stayed in Youngstown, we wouldn't have had the same opportunities. That move made all the difference in our lives.

Dad got a job in the furniture department at Fedco (Federal Employees Distributing Company), a store/company that can be seen as an early version of Target. Around 1971, Dad was no longer working at Fedco. He was a parking enforcer at UCLA. He would drive around in a little vehicle and give tickets to anyone illegally parked.

At that time, I lived in an apartment off campus. One evening, he dropped by to say hello. When he came in, I introduced him to Rudy, a friend from Colombia. When they saw each other, both Rudy and my dad had the strangest look on their faces, but nobody said anything, so I thought it was just my imagination. But it wasn't. A few days later, Dad gave me an explanation. A few days earlier, just when Dad was putting a ticket on the windshield of Rudy's car, Rudy arrived. He was furious and threatened to use his car to run over Dad, to which Dad replied, "Go ahead!" No wonder they were both so startled to find themselves together in my apartment.

In 1980, Dad was diagnosed with cancer. I flew home and was able to be with him for a few days before he passed. To describe my father, I'd like to add some other adjectives: kind and gentle; big-hearted; forgiving; magnanimous. In his will, dad left $1,500 (about $5,700 today, 2024) for my mother. When they divorced, dad was terribly hurt, but years later, holding no resentment, he remembered his former wife in his will.

Not everyone can be so forgiving. There's the story of a young woman who went to a florist to buy a cactus to send to the man who had just dumped her. The florist asked if she would like to include a card and say something. She said, "Yes. Sit on it!"

# CHAPTER 4

# MY MATERNAL GRANDPARENTS

**My maternal grandmother was Dina Bruder** Rothberg Aron Schulman. Her maiden name was Bruder. She was married three times. She was born in 1893, in Trok, a small Russian town in what is now Lithuania. She was the youngest of eleven children.

Her father (my great grandfather) had red hair, which he passed on to my mother, my Uncle Norman, my Aunt Lil, me, and several of my cousins. We redheads are in good (and sometimes infamous) company: Winston Churchill (British prime minister); Napoleon (French emperor); George Washington (US president); Mark Twain (US author and humorist); and Christopher Columbus (Italian explorer).

In the summer of 1909, when she was not quite sixteen, she left Trok, made it to Antwerp, Belgium, boarded a ship, and a few weeks later arrived in New York. It was a 3,000-mile voyage of seasickness and unsanitary conditions. But gaining entrance to America, as one immigrant recalled, "was as if God's great promise had been fulfilled."

Once beyond the gateway of Ellis Island, though, immigrants found that life could be every bit as hard as it had been back home. One immigrant put it this way: "I came to America because I heard the streets were paved with gold.

When I got here, I found out three things: First, the streets weren't paved with gold. Second, they weren't paved at all. Third, I was expected to pave them."

She didn't exactly go alone: a few people ahead of her in the immigration line on arrival in New York was an eighteen-year-old Jewish man also from Trok. As my cousin Eric Chevlen (our family genealogist) put it, "What a gutsy kid our grandmother was. She eloped to America with her sweetheart when she was sixteen years old and never looked back."

That man was Sam Rothberg. Two years later, he would become my grandmother's first husband. Sam Rothberg was born in Russia (Lithuania was then part of the Russian Empire) in 1892. My grandmother and Sam were married in Cleveland, Ohio, in 1911 (and four years later they moved to Youngstown). She wasn't quite eighteen, and he was nineteen. At the beginning of their marriage, Sam was a butcher, but by the time of his death in March of 1916, at age twenty-four from pulmonary tuberculosis, his butcher business had evolved into a small grocery store.

My grandmother's second husband was also named Sam. Sam Aron was born in 1894 in Vilna, today Vilnius, the capital of Lithuania. He immigrated to the US a few years after my grandmother. Sam Aron and my grandmother married in 1916, about seven months after the death of her first husband, Sam Rothberg. Whether she married for love, or convenience, or a combination, we don't know. At the time, she was a 23-year-old widow with three children under the age of four.

What was Sam Aron like? He was a devoted husband and father, a hard worker, and perhaps a little stern. He didn't like laughter at the table. Anyone who laughed had to go under the table, and it wasn't unusual to find most of the kids under the table before dinner was over. Sam belonged to a conservative Jewish congregation (Ohev Tzedek) and kept kosher.

Sam Aron joined my grandmother in the grocery business that she had established with her first husband, Sam Rothberg. Their marriage produced another six children. By the time she was forty, my grandmother was the mother of nine children, ranging in age from newborn to twenty-one years: Edward Rothberg Aron (1912–1968); Mary Rothberg Aron (1914–1992); Harry Rothberg Aron (1916–1996); Lillian Aron (1917–2000); Jules Aron (1919–2000); Rose Aron (1921–2013); Helen Aron (1922–2014); Norman Aron (1925–2018); and Audrey Aron (1933–2019).

By the end of 1936, they (my grandmother and Sam Aron) were reasonably successful. Their grocery business was doing well, and they toasted in the new year of 1937 with hopes for a bright future.

A month later, Sam was dead. Stricken with influenza, which developed into pneumonia, Sam died on January 27, 1937, at the age of forty-two. My grandmother had been married to Sam Rothberg for five years and then to Sam Aron for twenty-one years. She was to find love one more time. This marriage would last for twenty-four years, the rest of her life.

Harry Schulman (1893–1974) was born in Czarist Russia in what is modern-day Belarus. He served in the Czar's army in World War I and was captured by the Germans when his horse was shot out from under him. He was then forced to work on a prison farm. At the close of the war, he learned that his family in Russia had been murdered by the Bolsheviks. He spoke German well and had no reason to return to Russia, so he stayed in Germany.

Even before World War II officially began, the war against the Jews was in full force. Harry's wife died (December 1936) because it was forbidden for an Aryan doctor to attend to a sick Jew. Harry was incarcerated in the Dachau concentration camp, but before that he managed to get his daughter (my future Aunt Sonja) into a private Jewish boarding school, from which she was eventually transported to an orphanage (and luckily not to a death camp).

Before and at the beginning of the Second World War, Russia and Germany were allies, and Harry was technically still a Russian citizen. Indomitable and fearless twelve-year-old future Aunt Sonja (b. 1927) obtained an affidavit of sponsorship from the Pianin family in Youngstown, and confronted the Gestapo, saying they couldn't hold her dad because he was a Russian citizen. Harry was released from the concentration camp, and they escaped from Germany on the last boat to leave before the invasion of Poland in 1939.

Sometime in 1940, Harry met my grandmother, who was an attractive widow of forty-seven years. They married in 1941 in Youngstown, Ohio. Harry and Sonja joined my grandmother and her kids. While Sam Aron was my biological grandfather, he died many years before I was born. So when I think of my maternal grandfather, I think of Harry Schulman.

Sadly, I don't have many memories of Grandma and Grandpa Schulman. The sound of their voices is lost somewhere far back in my memory. I remember Grandma Schulman as being dignified, elegant, and often wearing a mink stole. My cousin Eric remembers her as a mature woman who "walked with a gait better described as strutting than walking."

# CHAPTER 5

# MY PATERNAL GRANDPARENTS

My paternal grandparents were **Marcus Isador** Silverstein (1874–1948) and Bertha Stern Silverstein (1884–1971). They were both born in Romania. When I think of Romania, two things immediately come to mind: spooky castles and Dracula, a vampire in the Bram Stoker novel of that name who lived in the Romanian region of Transylvania.

I first met Dracula (so to speak) in the horror film in which the vampire was immortalized by the Hungarian-American actor Bela Lugosi (1882–1956) with his iconic and unforgettable heavy Transylvanian accent. Horror films were in vogue when I was growing up. Who can forget Frankenstein, played by Boris Karloff (1887–1969), walking stiffly with arms outstretched? I don't remember if I was scared by these films or if I just thought of them as fun entertainment.

Bertha came to the United States in 1896 at the age of eleven or twelve. Marcus came in 1901 at the age of twenty-seven. They were married in 1903. Bertha would have been nineteen, and Marcus, twenty-nine. They had five children: Israel Silverstein (1903–1969); Ruth Silverstein Axelrad (1904–1987); Mildred Silverstein (1907–1908); David Silverstein Silvers (my dad, 1914–1980); Freda Silverstein Brodsky Gould (1917–2003).

In the early 1900s, they were living in Fort Dodge, Iowa, which at the time had a population of around 12,000. Compare that to other cities: San Francisco (340,000); Chicago (1,700,000); New York (3,000,000); and even Youngstown, Ohio, where my maternal grandparents settled (44,000). So Fort Dodge was really quite small.

My grandparents had a clothing store, Model Clothing Co. A 1903 newspaper ad from their store for underwear shows a man in fancy underwear standing in front of a dresser. He's being assisted by a young Afro-American dressed in livery. Today such an ad would be considered racist, but certainly my grandparents were unaware of the racial implications of the ad.

Growing up, I had some experiences with racism. When I was about ten (1957/1958), in Youngstown, I had two friends, brothers, who lived on a nearby block. One day, they said that there was going to be a meeting of the families on the block to talk about a problem. When I asked what the problem was, they said a Black family wanted to buy a house on the street. I have no idea what the meeting resulted in. I remember not understanding why that should be a problem.

With one exception, my friends were all white. It wasn't that I chose white over black; there were no Black families on Youngstown's north side where we lived. As I said, there was one exception. In high school, in the 9th grade, when I was fifteen, I had a Black friend, Dosier Taylor. After class, he would come over to my house, and we would work out with a set of barbells I had and then run around the block.

My parents objected and tried to tell me I shouldn't be having him over to the house. That was 1962. If it had been some years later, my parents certainly wouldn't have objected.

Of this, I am certain. But life in the United States was different in 1962. I didn't obey my parents, and Dosier and I continued working out for a year or so. In my memory, that was the only time I ever disobeyed my parents (such a good son!).

I never knew my paternal grandfather; he died less than a year after I was born. Although my grandfather was in the clothing business (and was rather short. Five feet six inches), he could've been a professional baseball player. He could've been the first Romanian-American all-star pitcher.

So what makes me say that? I will explain. One day my grandfather was at work in his clothing store. A stranger came in, and my grandfather became suspicious. When the man started to leave, my grandfather, suspecting he had stolen something, called out for the man to stop. He didn't comply, so my grandfather picked up a shoe and hurled it at the man, striking him in the head and knocking him to the floor. What a pitch! My grandfather then pulled open the man's coat, exposing the three pairs of pants he had tried to steal.

Sometime around 1930, my grandparents moved from Iowa to California and started a new business, a furniture store. Maybe this is where my father learned to make furniture. (I suspect they made the furniture they sold, but I am not sure.)

My first memory of Grandma Bertha is from the summer of 1964, when we moved from Youngstown to Los Angeles. My dad flew out first, and I followed a few months later. My dad picked me up at the airport, and we went straight to see my grandmother, who was living in Venice, a Los Angeles beach neighborhood. In the 1950s and the 1960s, Venice was characterized by low-rent, run-down bungalows inhabited by immigrants from eastern Europe, counterculture artists, poets, and writers.

When I met her that day, my grandmother was about eighty. She was living on the beach, but not in what I'd call a bungalow. It was more like a shack. Later, my dad and his sister, my Aunt Ruth, were able to move her into a nursing home.

The last time I saw Grandma Bertha, I was seventeen, and she was eighty-one or eighty-two. She was living in that nursing home. I had a bicycle, and I rode it to visit her. (I know. Those who know me will find it hard to believe that I once had a bicycle, and even harder to believe that I could actually keep my balance on one. More about my bike riding skills—or lack of them—in story # 7, Bro.)

I went in the early afternoon, but she was sleeping. I woke her up, and we had a short conversation (of which I remember nothing). She died in 1971 at the age of eighty-seven. Sadly, I never had much contact with my grandmother. Of course, today there's so much I would like to have asked her, but then I was a typical teenager, and it never occurred to me.

CHAPTER 6

# MO

**My sister Maureen's nickname is Mo.** It came about as a shortened version of her name, but I never called her that. When I hear the name Mo, what comes to mind has nothing to do with my sister. It brings to mind Moe Howard (1897–1975) of the Three Stooges. As a child, I enjoyed watching The Three Stooges with their antics and slapstick comedy.

My first memory of Maureen (b. 1949) was in California, around 1953. Our family was at the beach. As I started to go into the water, she began to cry. It isn't easy to think you're going to lose your six-year-old brother when you're about four and a half years old.

In 1954, we moved to Ohio. When we were growing up in Ohio (1954 to 1964), we had chores. We were in our early teens. One of my chores was a joint chore with Maureen. She would wash the dishes (no dishwasher), and my job was to dry the dishes. She would be in front of the sink washing, and I would be behind her, waiting with my towel. Now comes the fun part. I would hold two opposite corners of the towel, twist the towel, and flick it at her … at her … Well, you get the idea. For some reason she didn't think this was funny. How sad to be an unappreciated brother!

In 1964, our family moved to California. Maureen

graduated from Grant High School in 1967. That year she was elected prom queen and runner-up to homecoming queen. But Maureen was (and still is) another kind of queen. (No. Not a Drag Queen.) Just like ABBA's 1976 hit, she is a *Dancing Queen.* When Maureen was seven, she performed *Me and My Shadow* for a luncheon at our synagogue, imitating Mom's dance moves as if she were Mom's shadow. And she's been dancing ever since. Today (June of 2022), at age seventy-three, she still takes dance classes, and I mean classes that have strenuous movements. I hope I'll be that active when I reach seventy-three. Hey, wait a minute. I just remembered something: I'm almost two years older than she is!

Maureen also did some theater. While a student at Los Angeles Valley College, she was in *The Wizard of Oz.* The student director wanted her to play the title role of Dorothy. Maureen said, "But I can't sing." The director said, "Sure you can," had her sing *Somewhere Over the Rainbow,* realized that Judy Garland Maureen was not, and said, "How would you like to be a Munchkin?" It was a good fit, actually perfect. The Munchkins sang and danced as a group in lively choreographic sequences that included *We Welcome You to Munchkin Land, Ding-Dong! The Witch is Dead,* and *You're Off to See the Wizard.*

Theater runs in my family. My mother performed in several plays at the Youngstown Playhouse. And I once performed in a play. In 1963, during my junior year at Rayen High School, I was in *Our Town.* I only had a few lines, but it was an unforgettable experience: I forgot one of my lines! I was in the wrong play. I should've been in *The Play that Goes Wrong* (a 2012 play about the mishaps of an ill-fated theater company). My granddaughters have both performed in various plays or musicals at their schools. Giovanna played the part of Bert in the musical *Mary Poppins* at her junior high school, and Isabella was in several performances at her high school, Seattle Lakeside.

Maureen also writes poetry. Here are the first two stanzas of a poem she wrote when she was a student at Los Angeles Valley College (around 1968):

Anchored within the prisms of time
Stands a child;
A scrawny kid with a crooked grin,
Exhibiting two missing teeth.
His face is the portrait of mankind
And in his eyes wade the people of the world…

Youth, it is time to embark,
Leave the worn trails of the past
Where they transcend
The heights of felicitous growth
And seek the unknown.

Maureen has a big heart. She's always thinking about the well-being of others (it's thanks to her that my kids were able to come and live in the US). She's compassionate and empathetic. Once she paid for some groceries at a supermarket for someone whose card wasn't going through. (After that, I always invited her to go with me to the supermarket. And she thought it was because I liked her company.)

Maybe this (her sense of empathy) explains why she's a hugger (or maybe Freud can explain). Maureen loves (I mean really LOVES) to give hugs. Maureen isn't just a hugger; she's a serial hugger (well, at least she isn't a serial killer—that is, as far as I know). One Christmas, Maureen was working as a greeter at TJ Maxx. There was a long line. In that line there was a young woman in her mid-twenties who seemed to be sad. Maureen approached her and asked her if she would like a hug. She said she would. Then her friend said she would also like one. Then a shy ten-year-old girl asked for one. Then one by one, she gave a hug (upon request) to everyone in the line.

That was a lot of hugs, but the most hugs given (in twenty-four hours) is 9,277 by Jeffrey Ondash (US) at Bally's Hotel in Las Vegas in 2013. And the longest hug ever? That honor goes to Joe Snape and Will Jarvis, who embraced for 36 hours, 36 minutes, and 36 seconds. I would never participate in a hugging contest, unless, unless—unless it was with Dolly Parton.

And today (2024)? Maureen and Joel live in Huntington Beach, California, with their dog, Teddy. I'm not sure why they chose the name "Teddy." In honor of Teddy Roosevelt (US President)? Ted Bundy (serial killer)? Ted Hughes (English poet)? The teddy bear that came to life in the film *Ted?* I vote for Ted Hughes. Maureen was a poet herself, and she studied English literature in college. Joel is a retired radiologist (and a black belt in taekwondo). Their son, Daniel (b. 1985), is a manager in an auto parts store and lives nearby.

CHAPTER 7

# BRO

**Bro is an informal word for brother, a slang term** used as a friendly way of addressing a man or an adolescent boy: "Hey, bro, what's up?" Today I never use slang. However, as a teenager/college student in the late sixties, I did.

Here's some 60s slang I used: *Far Out* (amazing); *Gas* (a fun event); *Pad* (house or apartment); *Split* (to leave); *Crash* (to sleep at someone's place); *Don't flip your wig* (don't be upset); *foxy* (sexually attractive girl); *Beats me* (I don't know); *Bent out of shape* (angry); *Blow your mind* (something that amazes you); *Bread* (money); *Bummer* (disappointing); *Chick* (a young woman); *No sweat* (OK).

I'm three years older than Jeff (b. 1951). Often a younger sibling looks up to an older sibling. Maybe he did look up to me when we were both kids, but now that we're adults, I'm the one who looks up to him.

Our "unbiased" mother once said that Jeff is a "doctor's doctor," that is, a doctor who's so good that other doctors go to him or her when they have a patient with symptoms they're having trouble diagnosing or treating. Mom's words are even truer today. Today (2024), Jeff is Medical Director for Infection Control and Pharmacy at Sutter Health, a health care system in northern California with twenty-four acute-care hospitals and over two hundred clinics.

Jeff is competent (beyond competent), poised, calm, and self-assured, and despite his high-level position at Sutter, quite unassuming. For example, one day he was having lunch in the hospital cafeteria when suddenly, at a nearby table, someone began to choke. Jeff went over, applied the Heimlich maneuver, saved the young lady's life, and then calmly walked back to his seat as if nothing out of the ordinary had happened, as if he had just walked over to the other table to say hello to someone he hadn't seen for a couple of years.

Between 1954 and 1964, we lived in Youngstown, Ohio. Our parents bought a piano, and I started piano lessons with Mrs. Mary Schetzel. I was around ten, and Jeff was seven. I didn't have any desire to learn to play the piano. One day, as I was halfheartedly practicing, Jeff climbed onto the piano bench, nudged me aside (probably pushed me off), and began to play the piano.

Our family didn't have money for piano lessons, but Mrs. Schetzel said Jeff was so promising that she would give him lessons for free as long as he really dedicated himself to practicing. He would have to practice four hours every day. So, Jeff would practice two hours before he went to school and then another two hours after school. Now that's discipline and dedication!

In 1955, my Uncle Ed had a stroke. Around 1960, we moved from our house on Norwood to a duplex on Elm Street, and Uncle Ed rented a house across the street from us. He was unable to care for himself, so he had a full-time caretaker. Jeff (age nine) would go over to Uncle Ed's and read the newspaper to him, especially the business and financial section. Looking back, I wish I had also done that.

Uncle Ed and his brothers (Jules, Norman, and Harry) were successful businessmen. They were owners of Century Foods, a well-known local chain of grocery stores. I think that the daily contact with Uncle Ed rubbed off on Jeff. Why do I say that? Because around the time he began reading to Uncle Ed, Jeff opened his own store in front of our house. It was a kid's cardboard play store, and he sold things like candy and school supplies (pencils, notebooks).

We (the extended family) all admired Jeff's "little business venture." But there was someone who wasn't at all happy with it. That person was Abe, the owner of a corner store about one block away. He complained that Jeff's store was an unfair competition that was taking business away from him.

Jeff was the adventurous one of the three of us. In 1970, Jeff and a friend rode their bikes from Los Angeles to San Francisco, a distance of about four hundred miles as the crow flies. But since they weren't crows, their trip was closer to five hundred miles. It took them seven days to get to San Francisco. They traveled on California State Route 1, a long and winding scenic road with steep inclines that runs along the Pacific Coast. It's one thing to go up and down steep hills in a car and quite another to do it on a bicycle. Before making the trip, Jeff trained by riding his bike some forty miles every day over some of the steepest canyon roads in Los Angeles.

Not long after he got back, I asked him if I could take a spin on his bike. He said, "Sure. But be careful. I don't want anything to happen TO MY BIKE." I told him not to worry, got on the bike, peddled twice, and fell off, fracturing my thumb. Just when I was thinking about competing in the Tour de France!

Sometimes I wonder if Jeff and I are really related. Jeff can fix anything that goes wrong in his house. Garbage disposal or dishwasher not working? No need to buy a new one. Jeff can take care of it. Problem with the toilet or sink? No need to call a plumber (and sell your kidney to pay his bill). Room needs painting? Cabinet needs repaired? You get the idea. Whatever needs repaired, Jeff can handle it. Likewise, my son-in-law, Thomas, can repair anything. In fact, Thomas even designed and built an eight-by-ten-foot shed in the backyard (and I was as nervous as a long-tailed cat in a room full of rocking chairs as I watched him working on the roof). Me? I can change a light bulb, but only if it isn't too high!

And today (2024)? Jeff and Mindy live in Danville, California, about thirty miles from San Francisco. Mindy's a retired nurse, but Jeff (age seventy-two) really loves his job at Sutter Health and doesn't seem to have retirement in his near future plans. He continues "working like a dog." He's one of the two hardest working people I know (the other is my son-in-law, Thomas, who's a pharmacist at Children's Hospital in Seattle). Me? I prefer to be "hardly working" than to be "working hard." As Edgar Bergan said, "Hard work never killed anybody, but why take a chance?" (Edgar Bergan, 1903–1978, was a comedic ventriloquist whose puppet Charlie McCarthy wore a top hat, a tuxedo, and a monocle.)

Jeff and Mindy have three kids: Jason (b. 1985, a research and development chef for an international corporation); Heather (b. 1988, a nurse); and Casey (b. 1993, an independent contractor doing handyman work).

# CHAPTER 8

# THE THREE MUSKETEERS

In the 1844 novel *The Three Musketeers* by French author Alexandre Dumas (1802–1870), the three protagonists are remembered for saying, "All for one, and one for all!" If you say, "They are three musketeers," you mean those three people are united in friendship and will always be there for each other. My three kids, Paula (b. 1977), Sérgio (b. 1979), and David (b. 1985), are three musketeers. They're always helping each other. Always there for each other.

All three kids are doing well. Neusa would be all smiles with happiness and pride. I can say we did a good job (70% Neusa and 30% me; Okay. Probably 80% to my 20%).

We're a joking family. Sérgio always jokes, saying he's my favorite, and David says he's happy to be Number 2, as long as he isn't Number 3. Of course, I don't have a favorite. But the joke continues. I'm often the butt of a joke. The boys joke that when I was at Woodstock, I never saw a performance because I was too high. (For the record, I didn't go to Woodstock—but I wish I had—and I never did drugs.) And David recently reminded me that when he was a kid in Brazil and accompanied me to the mall, I would introduce him to my friends as "my little dog" and even ask him to bark.

Paula had a close relationship with her maternal

grandmother. Near her grandmother's house there was an outdoor market where the vendors sold fruits, vegetables, meats, and fish. Paula would accompany her grandmother and help her carry home the food items she bought.

Paula moved to the States in 2001. She shared an apartment with Sérgio (who was already living there) and his good friend from Manaus, Zé Neto, who had come to study English in Seattle. Soon after she arrived, Paula got a job at a drugstore, not far from the apartment they were renting. It was there that Paula met and began dating Thomas, who was a pharmacist at the drugstore. They were married on July 12, 2003.

In 2003, Paula got a job at the University of Washington as an administrative assistant to the president of the university. When Isabella (Isa) was born in 2005, Paula stopped working (just as her mother had done when she was born) to take care of her and later Giovanna (Gio), who was born in 2008.

Some years later, in 2013, Paula became friends with the mother of one of Isa's grade school classmates who offered her a part-time job in her law office as a paralegal. In 2016, Paula began working at the University of Washington in the physics department, as a program's assistant and then as an academic advisor. In March of 2024, she transferred to the Foster School of Business, where she's a senior academic counselor for nearly three hundred undergraduate students.

Sérgio was the most mischievous (impish, difficult) of the three. Actually, the only mischievous one. Once (I don't remember how old he was), he took a paperclip, unbent part of it, and used a rubber band to shoot it into my thigh when I wasn't looking. OUCH!!

When Paula's first boyfriend came over one evening and

they were seated on the sofa in the living room, Sérgio (age fourteen) walked into the room, sat down next to them (at least it wasn't between them), turned to him, and said (in Portuguese) "What are your intentions with my sister?"

In 2000, Sérgio went to live in the US, first with my sister and her family and then with his friend Zé Neto. In 2000, helped by his Uncle Joel, Sérgio got a job at Albertson's as a bag boy and later at Children's Hospital as a patient transporter. In 2006, he began working at Harborview, a public hospital known as a regional trauma center. In 2008 he graduated as a radiology technologist, and in 2015, he got certified as an MRI technologist.

In January of 2013, Sérgio went to the Philippines on vacation. There he met Angela Hwang, who was also there on vacation. Angela was born in Korea, but when she was three, her parents immigrated to Australia. When Sérgio met her, she had been living in Korea. Sérgio came back from the Philippines but went to visit Angela in Korea in April. Angela came to the States in August, and they were married on November 9, 2013.

On March 6th of 2023, they became parents of twins, Leon and Rafael. Sérgio and Angela are doing an outstanding job as parents (as are Paula and Thomas). Neusa would be so proud of them (as I am). Twins aren't just double the work; they're a hundred times more work and stress. I told them that when they're having a bad day, they should think of my cousin Eric, who had two sets of twins within a year! and survived. (Okay, Laurel had the babies, with a little input—so to speak—from Eric.)

David has always been the calmest of the three. When he was about two, somehow he aspirated a bean into his nose. We had to go to several emergency rooms or clinics before we found a doctor who was able to get the bean out. I don't remember David even crying. Actually, it was quite dangerous because if the bean had gone down into his lungs, it could've been fatal.

Another two dramatic things happened to David. The first happened when he was about eight. We were at the home of one of Paula's friends. Since there was a swimming pool in the backyard, we told him to play in the front yard. He went towards the street and fell into an open sewer! Luckily, somehow he managed to crawl up and out. He could've died, disappeared, and we never would've known what had happened.

The second happened when he was sixteen. One evening, while waiting for his bus near the mall, he was held up by a street urchin holding a revolver. He told David to hand over his wallet, which he did. David then calmly asked him if he could at least give him back his bus fare, which he was "nice enough" to do.

David and Sérgio shared a room in Manaus and were very close, even though there's a five-year age difference. Sergio would often practice judo holds on David and make him say, "Perdão meu Mestre," something like the American expression of "crying uncle." David would also serve as a human barbell. He would stretch out horizontally, and Sérgio would curl him like a barbell.

When Sérgio left for the States in 2000, David (age fifteen) was devastated. I remember him throwing himself on his bed and sobbing. A few years later (2003), David came to the States and roomed with Sérgio. Like Sérgio, David became a radiology technologist, and later an MRI technologist. And in fact, they now (2024) work together in the same University of Washington outpatient radiology department. (Double Trouble!)

In 2014, David was working at Northwest Hospital, where he met Mirella Mendoza, who is Mexican-American. Mirella's family lives in Medford, Oregon, an eight-hour drive from Seattle. David decided to go to Medford to ask Mirella's parents for their blessing to marry their daughter. Since Mirella's parents were born in Mexico, David did it in (broken) Spanish.

I drove with David and told her parents (in my rusty Spanish) that David was a sincere, trustworthy young man who would do everything to make Mirella happy and that I would welcome her into the family as a daughter. I finished by pointing to David and saying, "David es mi perrito" ("David is my little dog.") Old habits are hard to die.

David and Mirella were married on October 8, 2016, in Medford in a ceremony conducted in Spanish. Afterwards I went up to the priest and, in my broken Spanish, commented on the beautiful ceremony, adding that I had lived many years in Brazil and that in Brazil we say, "Español es Portugués malhablado" (Spanish is Portuguese badly spoken). To this day, I'm not sure if the priest understood I was making a joke.

Maybe I need to find some new jokes. Maybe I should borrow some jokes from American comedian Joan Rivers (1933– 2014). Here are a few from her:

- My best birth control now is just to leave the lights on.

- I don't exercise. If God had wanted me to bend over, he would have put diamonds on the floor.

- Don't talk to me about Valentine's Day. At my age, an affair of the heart is a bypass.

# PART TWO:

# FIRST MEMORIES

# (YOUNGSTOWN

# AND LA)

# CHAPTER 9

# MY EARLIEST MEMORY

There's a saying, "A house is not a home." It means a "house" is just a physical structure, while a "home" is lived-in and full of memories with (usually) positive connotations, such as family, love, happiness, and belonging (unless you come from a broken home).

Over my lifetime, I've lived in a number of different houses/or apartments (physical structures), and in each case it was a "home" filled with happy memories. In this memoir, I'm going to revisit some of the memories I associate with each of those houses or apartments. Before we look at my first memory, let's look at some "houses" in famous literary works.

- **THE HOUSE ON MANGO STREET.** 1984. By Mexican-American author Sandra Cisneros. It tells the story of Esperanza Cordero, a twelve-year-old Chicana girl growing up in the Hispanic quarter of Chicago.

- **A HOUSE IS NOT A HOME.** 1953. The memoir of Pearl "Polly" Adler, a famous American madam whose "house of ill repute" was frequented by such notables as Desi Arnaz of *I Love Lucy* fame; comedian Milton Berle; New York City mayor Jimmy Walker; gossip columnist Walter Winchell; and mobster Dutch Schultz.

- **LITTLE HOUSE ON THE PRAIRIE.** 1935. An autobiographical children's novel by Laura Ingalls Wilder, recounting her adolescent experiences while growing up in a one-room log cabin in Indian Territory on the Kansas prairie around 1869.

The first house of which I have a memory was in Youngstown, Ohio (1952), and I was five years old. It was a two-story brick building, with two steps from the lawn to the front door. In my memory, I'm standing on the top step, peeing onto the lower steps. My father sees me and informs me that I should come in and use the toilet.

Why I should have this particular memory only Freud can explain. I wasn't training to be an exhibitionist. Which reminds me of something that occasionally happened during my university days. Around 1970, there was a new fad at American universities, a fad that could be described as crazy, daring, provocative, and (for my parents' generation) shocking.

What fad could that be? I'll give you a clue. It wasn't seeing how many bored, brainless college students could be stuffed into a Volkswagen Beetle. That fad began in 1959 and peaked in the mid-1960s when a record eighteen people stuffed themselves into one. (I never tried it, but I imagine it could've been "fun" depending on who was stuffed in next to me, if you know what I mean.)

The new fad was "streaking," which is the act of running naked through a public area. I never tried that either, but I do remember once being at dinner at Hershey Hall, the graduate student dorm, in spring of 1970, when a shapely student steaked through the dining hall, almost causing me to choke on my food.

Which reminds me of a little joke. Two eighty-year-old women were sitting on a park bench and saw a young girl streaking. One of them said, "I'm going to streak before I die." And with that, she took off her clothes and ran past two old men. The first old man said, "Did you see that?" And the other old man replied, "Whatever it is, it sure needs a lot of ironing."

While some of us "boomers" think of streaking as one of our contributions to the 1960s pop culture, the first recorded incident of streaking by a college student in the United States actually occurred in 1804 at Washington College (now Washington and Lee University) when senior George William Crump was arrested for running naked through Lexington, Virginia, where the university is located. Crump was suspended for the academic session but later went on to become a US Congressman, which reminds me of Mark Twain's quote: "Suppose you were an idiot, and suppose you were a member of Congress; but I repeat myself."

In 1974, recently married, I was back in the States finishing my master's in Spanish at UCLA. Neusa had heard my story about the streaking fad and wasn't amused. Then on came the news showing nurses in San Francisco on strike holding up large placards, saying "ON STRIKE." At the time, Neusa's English was still rather basic. She looked at the word "strike" and read it with the Portuguese rendering of those letters, which produced the word "streak." Her comment to me, in Portuguese: Even the nurses doing that craziness!

CHAPTER 10

# LOS ANGELES APARTMENT
# (1953)

In 1953, we moved to Los Angeles. I was five years old. We lived in an apartment on the ground floor. I have only a few vague memories from that time. My first memory of Christmas was from that apartment. Although we're Jewish, for some reason my parents decided we would celebrate Christmas that year, not in the spiritual sense but in having a tree with presents under the tree. I woke up early Christmas day, long before anyone else, and did what any five-year-old worth his salt would do: I opened all of the presents, mine, Jeff's, and Maureen's.

In the apartment next to ours, there was a kid named Rusty who was fourteen years old. I would sometimes go over to his apartment and watch him work out with a set of barbells. How grown-up and strong he was! (Remember, this was from the eyes of a five-year-old.) I couldn't even budge the barbells one inch off the ground, and yet he effortlessly lifted them over his head several consecutive times in what's known as an overhead press.

Years later, when I was his age or a little older, I would work out with weights at the Jewish Community Center in Youngstown, Ohio, in a failed effort to become a bodybuilder-turned-movie star like Steve Reeves (1926–2000), who was famous in the mid-1950s for starring in Italian-made sword-and-sandal films in which he played muscular protagonists, such as Hercules and Goliath (I grew up watching his films).

Besides Rusty, there was also a kid around my age. I don't remember his name, but I do remember he was a bully who used to run after me, hitting me on the back, as I fled to escape him. I have no idea what became of him, but I imagine he graduated from being a child bully to being a mafia hit man.

I also graduated from a tricycle to a regular bicycle, but with training wheels. There was a driveway entrance on one side of the building and a driveway exit on the other. Thus, I could ride my bike around the building, riding on the sidewalk for the part in front of the building. Pretty safe. The only problem is that nobody told me that it wouldn't be a good idea to ride my bike with my eyes closed. And a good idea it wasn't! No major injury, just a couple of bruises.

Riding my bike completely around the apartment building with my eyes closed would have been quite a feat, but it pales in comparison to the accomplishments of some extraordinarily talented and fearless blind individuals. Here are three of those incredible blind individuals: Derek Rabelo (a blind Brazilian surfer who has surfed Hawaii's board-breaking Banzai Pipeline, which is known for its huge deadly waves); Erik Weihenmayer (the first blind person to climb the Seven Summits—the highest mountain on each of the seven continents, which of course includes Everest); and Jacob W. Bolotin (1888–1924), the world's first totally blind physician.

# PART THREE:

# YOUNGSTOWN

# (1954-1964)

# CHAPTER 11

# GROWING UP IN A LARGE EXTENDED FAMILY

I was lucky to grow up in a large, close-knit extended family in Youngstown, Ohio, from ages eight to sixteen, until 1964 when we moved to Los Angeles. That experience, along with the Jewish Community Center and the Boy Scouts, provided me with a happy, untroubled, enjoyable, idyllic childhood.

My grandmother, Dina Bruder Rothberg Aron Schulman, was married three times. She had three children with her first husband, Sam Rothberg (Ed, Mary, and Harry), and six children with her second husband, Sam Aron (Lil, Jules, Rose, who was my mother, Helen, Norman, and Audrey). Her third husband (Harry Schulman) in 1941 added a stepdaughter, my Aunt Sonja, to the family.

When Sam Rothberg died in 1916, Uncle Ed was not yet four, Aunt Mary not quite three, and Uncle Harry slightly over a month old. That same year, Grandma married Sam Aron, who, according to my cousin Eric Chevlen, adopted her children "in fact, if not in law." Thus, this large extended family is known as "the Aron family."

Everyone lived in Youngstown, so I grew up surrounded by eighteen aunts and uncles and twenty-two cousins. Most of my cousins were around my age, so we were always together at birthday parties and other family functions. It was wonderful (incredible, fantastic, awesome; you get the idea) growing up with so many aunts, uncles, and cousins.

In my mind's nostalgic eye, I see a large, caring, loving, supportive, extended family, like the family portrayed in Norman Rockwell's 1943 *Saturday Evening Post* painting of a family celebrating Thanksgiving.

Or like the idealized, wholesome families portrayed in the 1950s/1960s sitcoms, such as *The Adventures of Ozzie and Harriet; Leave it to Beaver; The Andy Griffith show; My Three Sons;* and *Father Knows Best,* TV shows that presented family values of respect and getting along, and where all of life's minor but normal problems, complications, predicaments, and disappointments can be solved by a good talk from father and a batch of cookies from mother.

So what was it like growing up in this large extended family? Perhaps my cousin Judi Zoldan's memories will give you a feel for what it was like:

> "Grandma Schulman's holiday dinners, everyone together; Talks with Uncle Jules; Scrambled eggs on Saturday night with Linda, Joyce, and Gary; Aunt Bert teaching me how to knit; Eating bologna sandwiches with the Silvers after Sunday school; Planning my fall wardrobe with Linda and Maureen; The wonderful surprise of Uncle Norman coming with his convertible, top down, the car filled with cousins for a trip to buy ice cream."

In the Aron family, there was one family member who stood out, who was the prime mover, the glue that held the extended family together. That member was Uncle Norman

(1925–2018). Uncle Norman was the one who, in the words of Cousin Judi, "brought all the family together for pure delight and fun."

Early on, Uncle Norman showed his dedication to family. One day, while still a teenager, Uncle Norman went to visit his sister (my Aunt Lil) and found her washing clothes by hand. Several hours later, he came back with a washing machine. At an age when most teens are worried about their pimples, their "crushes," or their upcoming math test for which they "forgot to study," Uncle Norman worried about his older sister.

In 1945, Aunt Mary, Uncle Bill, and Cousin Sheldon were living in California. It was the end of World War Two. Sheldon was six or seven. Uncle Norman, who was just twenty years old, sent him a box of Double Bubble Gum. All of Cousin Sheldon's classmates and friends wanted Uncle Norman for their uncle!

Whenever there was a need, Uncle Norman was there to help, providing love, guidance, and, at times, financial support to ensure happiness and stability. When my parents got divorced in 1968, Uncle Norman flew down to Los Angeles to help us deal with that crisis. When our world was sinking, in turmoil, Uncle Norman came to help us find our way forward. Uncle Norman's support to us, and especially to our mother (his sister), was beyond special, beyond compare; its importance cannot be overstated.

As Cousin Karen Zoldan said, Uncle Norman was "an exemplar of what it means to be a truly good human being."

CHAPTER 12

# NORWOOD

**I lived in Youngstown from 1954 to 1964** (ages eight to sixteen), when we moved to California. I lived in two houses in Youngstown (well, not at the same time). The first was on Norwood and the second on Elm Street.

The house on Norwood was two stories tall, not counting a basement and an attic, wooden, gray in color, and had a front porch. My mother used the attic to practice her dancing. The basement was Dad's shop, where he built furniture for our house and for some of my aunts and uncles.

Upstairs, there were three bedrooms and a bathroom. Jeff and I shared a bedroom (this was before he was old enough to know and complain about what a messy brother he had). Maureen had her own bedroom with two twin beds, one against the wall and the other in front of the window. Occasionally, I would sleep in Maureen's room, lying on my back with my feet propped up against the wall. (Very relaxing. Was I doing yoga at age eight?)

You don't expect to have many memories, if any, associated with a bathroom. But actually there is a memory associated with the bathroom in the house on Norwood: Cousin Judi (maybe six at the time) locked herself in the bathroom and couldn't figure out how to open the door. Mom had to call the fire department to come and "rescue" her.

Actually, there are several historic events associated with bathrooms. Here is one:

**SAVED BY A BATHROOM BREAK.** In 1942, future US President Lyndon B. Johnson (1902–1973) had to use the bathroom just before his combat mission was about to take off. When he came out, another soldier had taken his place and was on the flight, which was shot down by the Japanese, killing all on board.

Every evening, I would spread out the newspaper on the rug on the floor in the living room. I didn't read all the news (and never the sports page), but without fail I read the funnies. Some popular funnies of the 1950s include *Beetle Bailey; Blondie; Dick Tracy; Little Orphan Annie; Li'l Abner; Nancy; Henry; Peanuts;* and *Dennis the Menace* (who I have reason to believe was reincarnated as my son Sérgio).

But I wasn't the only one to appreciate the *Youngstown Vindicator.* We had just gotten a puppy, and once when I got up to go to the bathroom, I returned to find that the puppy had also gone to the bathroom: on the newspaper I had left on the floor.

Our dog was a wire-haired fox terrier, which we named "Asta" after the dog of that breed from the 1957–1959 television series *The Thin Man*. Asta might have been cute and well-behaved on television, but ours was full of energy, required constant attention, peed where it shouldn't, humped the sofa cushions, and barked incessantly. Actor Humphrey Bogart (1899–1957) and poet Rudyard Kipling (1865–1936) also had fox terriers, but that doesn't change my opinion: a fox terrier is the perfect gift for the child of your "frenemy." (If you can't find a fox terrier, a trumpet would produce the same results.)

At that time, our family had a maid, Loretta, a young 24-

year-old Negro (the term from that era; today she would be called "an African-American" or a "person of color"). My memories of Loretta are pleasant but vague. When my parents were out for the evening, Loretta would disregard my bedtime curfew and let me stay up and watch *Gun Smoke* (one of the best-known and longest-running TV westerns) with her on the television downstairs.

We had another maid. The only thing I remember is that she was Chinese and once ran after me with a broom and didn't catch me because I crawled under the dining room table. I don't remember the outcome of this situation. All I know is President Eisenhower (in office 1953–1961) should've called the American ambassador back from China in protest.

In the backyard there were two cherry trees, which me and my friends (ages around ten or eleven) would climb. I didn't climb up very high, but some of my friends went way up. This brings to mind the 1967 Fifth Dimension hit *Up, Up, and Away*, one of my favorite songs, which was about a balloon and not a tree. I didn't go "up, up, and away," but I did go up high enough to get some ripe cherries.

When I was eleven, I became interested in astronomy. My parents bought me a small telescope, and many an evening I would lie on the grass in the front yard (even when the yard was covered with snow) and peer through it at the moon, the stars, and planets. That year, 1959, I became the youngest member of the Youngstown Astronomy Club.

The front yard was covered in grass and also had some kind of small plant that attracted bees, and the bees attracted me and my friends. We would take an empty glass peanut butter jar, punch a few small holes in the lid, remove the lid, and put the jar down over a bee that was visiting some clover. When the bee flew to the top of the jar, we cautiously raised the jar from the ground and quickly put the lid on the jar, capturing the bee. We soon had a jar full of angry buzzing bees.

I don't remember ever being stung, but I'm sure it's something that Johannes Relleke of Zimbabwe (then Rhodesia) will never forget. In 1962, he was stung an incredible 2,443 times (and survived).

Winters were cold, and the ground was covered with snow. When I was around ten, we would build snowmen and snow forts and have snowball fights. Even when we were older and in high school, we would throw snowballs at each other, sometimes with unintended results. Once, one of us threw a snowball at a friend. The friend ducked, and the snowball hit the mother of another friend (Dickie Friedman) who had just rolled down her window to shout something to her son. Instead, she shouted at us. I don't remember what she said, which is probably just as well.

I had a group of friends my age (between ten and twelve) I played with. My closest friend was Jimmy Witt. We would shoot baskets, play catch with a hard ball, and throw a football back and forth. We also played in the street. We played Simon Says, Hide and Seek, Cowboys and Indians, and Three Feet in the Mud Gutter. Back then (late 1950s), it was safe to play in the street (there was little traffic), and it was safe to be out in the early evening. Sadly, that probably is no longer true today.

Finally, if we found an empty pack of Lucky Strike cigarettes (a popular brand at the time, along with Marlboro), whoever first saw the pack would hit the person nearest him and say, "Lucky Strike and no strikes back!"

# CHAPTER 13

# ELM STREET

Around July of 1960 (me age twelve), we moved from our house on Norwood to a house on Elm Street. Luckily, it was before Freddy Krueger got there and became famous when a film about him (*A Nightmare on Elm Street*) was made in 1984.

Freddy didn't make a good first impression and probably would've had a hard time getting a date: he had a burned, disfigured face, wore a dirty red-and-green-striped sweater and a brown fedora, and had a metal-clawed, right-hand glove. (This was before internet dating sites where you can post a fake picture and a charming but false profile.) I'm glad he wasn't my neighbor. True to his looks, he wasn't a nice guy: his ghost haunted and killed some teenagers in their dreams (slashing them to death with his clawed hand), causing their deaths in the real world as well.

I'm also glad I never saw the film. Not my kind of film. I prefer films like *Francis, the Talking Mule* (an army mule that talks to a young soldier); *Abbott and Costello Meet Frankenstein; Road to Morocco* (Bob Hope, Bing Crosby, and Dorothy Lamour); *Young Frankenstein;* and *The Pink Panther.*

It was a good location. A few blocks from Rayen high school (which I began a few months later as a freshman), and a few blocks from Aunt Helen and Uncle Harold. Also, it wasn't too many blocks to Rodef Sholom Temple, where my Boy Scout troop met every Thursday evening.

Our house was a two-story brick building. We had the downstairs, and the owner had the upstairs. We had three bedrooms, a bathroom, a living room/dining room, a small kitchen (which had a small table to take informal meals), and a small den.

I shared a bedroom with my brother. One of us was neat and liked everything in its place; the other was the opposite, messy and completely disorganized, clothes on the floor, nothing in its proper place. I'd like to say that I was the neat one, but that would be a lie. Since I am trying to tell my life story as truthfully as possible, I must reluctantly admit I was the messy one. In fact, I was so messy that my brother ran a cord across the room, dividing it in half, so that my mess would stay on my side of the room. Today, I'm neat and organized. When I wake up, the first thing I do is make my bed. (And if one morning I don't wake up, my bed will still be neat, but with me under the covers, covered up like a mummy, which is the way I sleep.)

I wonder if there's a gene for being messy which I passed on to my boys, Sérgio and David. When Neusa and I moved to the States in 2010, Sérgio and David were roommates renting an apartment together. When we first visited their apartment, we thought there had been a tornado in Seattle, more precisely a tornado that had only hit their apartment. Clothes, books, papers, and receipts strewn everywhere, on their bed, on the floor; the sink full of unwashed dishes. But if there's a gene for messiness, there's also a cure: marriage. Like me, after getting married, my boys miraculously stopped being messy.

I have a surprisingly fond memory associated with the

kitchen, a memory that has nothing to do with food. I say surprisingly fond because you don't usually associate a fond memory with a chore like washing the floor. Yes, one of my teenage chores was to wash the kitchen floor, which I did on my hands and knees, using a small bucket of soapy water and a rag.

I don't remember how my fifteen-year-old self felt about that "small obligation" (I probably wasn't thrilled, but I don't remember ever complaining), but my seventy-six-year-old self looks back fondly and is glad I was "given" that chore. (I certainly didn't spontaneously go up to my mother and say, "Mom, I've been thinking. Would you mind if I washed the kitchen floor?")

In the den there was a large varnished wooden wine barrel on top of which Dad had placed a large round plywood disk covered with orange Formica. In the center, he created a fountain that sent water onto a two-foot-tall imitation champagne bottle that had been used for advertising in a store or as a theater prop. Near the bottom there was a metal footrest encircling the barrel. This wine-barrel table was accompanied by a set of bar stools with orange seats matching the orange tabletop.

## CHAPTER 14

# COUSIN ERIC

**Our house on Elm Street had a small backyard** where me and my cousin Eric Chevlen (b. 1949) occasionally built a small fire and baked a cake (we were in Boy Scouts together), using the "Busy Day Cake" recipe from a Betty Crocker cookbook.

I'd like to say that our cakes were delicious (and to us they probably were; thirteen and fifteen-year-old boys aren't noted for their culinary discernment), but in reality, after sixty years, it's hard to say how they tasted. Probably "edible" would best describe them. If we had had a time machine, maybe we could've entered our creations in the *Great British Bake Off*, which debuted in 2010. (Presenter: "And now our next contestants are two lads from across the water.")

Eric is a poet with several published books of poems. Triple Crown (2010) is a set of interlocking, linked sonnets. They're not simple, easy-to-understand poems of the kind you find in the works of my favorite poet, British-Canadian Robert Service (1874–1958), known as "the Bard of the Yukon" and who was famous for poems such as "The Spell of the Yukon" and "The Shooting of Dan McGrew." Triple Crown is more in the tradition of British poet T. S. Eliot (1888–1965), whose poetry ("The Wasteland"; "The Love Song of J. Alfred Prufrock") is known for its complexity and difficulty, requiring extensive knowledge of history, literature, and philosophy.

Eric's most recent book is *Born to Blush Unseen: Collected and Rejected Poems* (2023). Referring to this book, with his wry sense of humor, he said, "This is my third published volume of poetry. My earlier works were received with widespread apathy. I expect no less from this book." Here's a poem from it. One I particularly like.

### A RUBA'I TO COMFORT MY DAUGHTER
Beyond the clouds of gloom or rain or snow,
The sun, beneficent, remains aglow,
And we shall bask again, for yet it shines
Beyond the cloud, if only we would know.

And one more.

Though draped in black the crow cannot foresee
How other crows will peck at his demise.
Likewise, the night-hid owl, though he is wise,
Asks who, who next, who next, though it is he.
The elephant, with famous memory,
Looks backward, never forward to his fall.
The moose, the mouse, all creatures great and small,
Are born, live unafraid, then cease to be.
Not so with us. Not so with *sapiens*,
Who borrows from tomorrow this day's dread,
And fills his life with death far in advance.
O pitiful, O Homo Trepidans,
Who waltzes through his life already dead,
And hears no music halfway through his dance.

This one is me. Many years ago, when my granddaughter Isa was eight years old, she gave me the nickname "Mr. Worry."

So, yes, I tend to worry, but nevertheless, I do hear and appreciate the "music" in my life.

Eric has read and studied the entire text of *The Talmud*, the primary source of Jewish religious and civil law, a project that took him seven and a half years to complete.

When I think of Eric's religious studies and his seven-year project of reading the Talmud, I'm reminded of one of my favorite (secular, humorous) authors, A. J. Jacobs, who wrote *The Year of Living Biblically* (which was his quest to spend a year following the Bible as literally as possible).

Eric sings in a barbershop quartet and has acted in community theater productions. My mother also acted in community theater some seventy years ago; she was a stripper in *Gypsie* and would be happy that her nephew is continuing the tradition (of acting, not of being a stripper. But it's not too late.).

Here are two fun stories about Eric.

- Once, when he was in high school, Eric went to a party, and when it was time to go home, he asked a friend for a ride. When he got home, his father said, "Eric, where's the car?" Eric had forgotten that he had driven to the party.

- The temple was having a book sale. Eric came home feeling overjoyed with the books he had acquired at a good price. When he showed them to Uncle Harold, my uncle said, "Eric, those are the same books I donated to the temple for the book sale."

Oh yes. I forgot to mention. Eric is a retired oncologist, who, for over thirty years, administered care and solace to his desperately ill patients. Kudos to you my dear cousin.

# CHAPTER 15

# HARDING AND HAYES

**Here are some memories from grade school** (Harding, third grade through sixth grade) and Hayes (seventh and eighth grades).

In 1954, I entered Harding Elementary School as a third-grader. The school was named after Warren G. Harding, president of the United States from 1921 to 1923. Harding was the first president to ride to his inauguration in an automobile and the first to own a radio. While president, he played poker twice a week and sneaked off to burlesque shows. His advisors were known as the "Poker Cabinet" because they all played poker together.

My third-grade teacher was Mrs. Pennal. All I remember is that she kept telling me to quit fidgeting. My fourth-grade teacher was Mrs. Dean. I remember her as a rather large woman and heavily perfumed. My fifth-grade teacher was Miss Grace Jones. She was strict but nice.

Sixth grade was the last year of elementary school, and my teacher was Mrs. Metz. In my desk, I had a little tin container full of spitballs. Whenever she went out of the room, we boys would have a spitball fight.

School should prepare students for their future. And strange as it may seem, those spitball fights did prepare me for an incident that would occur years later when I was in my junior year at UCLA. We can call it "the college version of a spitball fight." I was in the dorm dining hall. All of a sudden someone shouted, "Food fight," and flung a handful of food at students seated at another table. Within minutes, the whole cafeteria was a war zone, the air filled with edible missiles. Who said college students are more mature than a sixth-grader? (I didn't take part. I just hid under the table, like a good pacifist.)

Seventh and eighth grades were at Hayes Junior High, named after Rutherford Birchard Hayes (you can't invent a name like Rutherford Birchard!), president of the United States from 1877 to 1881. President Hayes was the first president to have a telephone and a typewriter in the White House. His wife was nicknamed "Lemonade Lucy" because she banned alcohol from the White House. There were a lot of animals in the Hayes White House: cows, five kittens, five dogs, five birds, a goat, and several horses. He chose the wrong profession. He should've been a veterinarian.

In Mrs. Metz's sixth grade class, we were never punished for the spitball fights, but it was a different story at Hayes Junior High. Misbehavior was punished by a paddling. The transgressor would be told to go to the front of the class or the hallway and bend over. The teacher would then smack him (for some reason it was always a boy) on the butt with a flat wooden board resembling a small tennis racket. OUCH! The teachers jokingly called this paddle "the board of education."

I only remember two classes at Hayes. The first was a subject called "health education." The only thing I remember from this class is the word "peristalsis" (the wave-like movement of your digestive muscles that moves food through your digestive tract). Yes, I've actually remembered that word over all of these years, and this is the first time I've had the opportunity to use it. I was never able to use it in a conversation. I never asked anyone, "How is your peristalsis today?" However, I sometimes use it when I am talking to myself. Whenever I'm a little constipated (luckily, not very often), I say to myself, "Come on, peristalsis. Do your stuff."

Music class came right after gym class, and that was a problem. There were no showers, so we came to class sweaty and smelly. It was winter. The windows were closed, and there was no air conditioning, just a fan. The room was hot and stinky.

The smell was awful, but there are things that smell worse than a classroom of twenty sweaty young teenagers, for example, vomit, a skunk, rotten eggs, and a flower called *Rafflesia Arnoldii*. This flower is known as the "Stinking Corpse Lily" because it smells like a dead, decaying, rotting corpse. But I had a solution. I brought a small jar of Vicks VapoRub and passed it around. Everyone rubbed a little bit on their nose to counteract the terrible smell in the room. And it worked.

There are many purported uses for Vicks, making it a medicinal version of a Swiss Army knife. Here are a few: treat acne; relieve headaches, sore muscles, and itchiness; fight against stretch marks; silence a squeaky door; promote hair growth; and even, Are you ready for this last one? even treat hemorrhoids (only for the bravest of the brave or the stupidest of the stupid).

# CHAPTER 16

# RAYEN HIGH SCHOOL

**In September of 1961, I began Rayen High** School in Youngstown, Ohio. I was thirteen years old (I would be fourteen in December) and was what is known as a freshman.

Rayen was named after Colonel William Rayen, a judge and former military officer who fought in the War of 1812 between the United States and Great Britain. When Judge Rayen died in 1854, he left money for the establishment of a secondary school, which was to be "free and open to students of all backgrounds."

Perhaps the most famous alumnus was Albert Warner, one of the founders of the Warner Bros. entertainment group and movie studio. In 1900, Warner was quarterback for Rayen's football team.

A number of famous people once played football in high school or college: actors Denzel Washington, Bill Cosby, and Will Ferrell; country music singers Garth Brooks and Willie Nelson; and US presidents Ronald Reagan, Richard Nixon, and Gerald Ford. (US president Lyndon Johnson once remarked that Gerald Ford was "a nice guy, but he played too much football with his helmet off.")

I remember Rayen as a big, cavernous, two-story building. I didn't have a very promising start. My grades for my first year: algebra (C); Latin I (B); English I (C); and ancient history (C).

My ancient history teacher was Mrs. Whan. I remember her talking about Mesopotamia, the Tigris and Euphrates Rivers, and the Cradle of Civilization, and as they say in the closings of the Loony Tunes cartoons, "That's all folks!" I don't remember anything else about her classes.

My Latin teacher was Miss Lucy Lee. I remember her as a thin, older woman. I really enjoyed her classes. I enjoyed learning Latin (*puella, puellae, puellae, puellam, puellā, puella—amō, amās, amat, amāmus, amātis, amant*). Miss Lee was a good teacher, and I think it was because of her Latin classes that I became interested in learning languages.

The next year, my sophomore year, my grades improved: English II (B); plain geometry (B); biology (B); Latin II (A). I must have developed some decent study habits, but that was no thanks to the school. Rayen didn't offer freshmen a course on how to study; they just expected the students to already possess that knowledge.

In September of 1963, I began my junior year. I distinctly remember an event that occurred on Friday, November 22, at around 2 o'clock in the afternoon. I was in Spanish class, listening to the teacher (Nicholas Cipollone) play a tape with dialogues from our coursebook. Another teacher knocked on the door and called him out. He came back in with a solemn, somber, sad face and told us that President Kennedy had just been assassinated. Class was dismissed, and we all went home to watch the news on our black-and-white televisions.

My physics teacher (John Petretich) was a rather short man. I don't remember him as being a particularly good teacher, and in fact, this caused me to do something I never should've done: I went to the principal's office and complained. The stupid things we do when we're young!

Years earlier, his son had a paper route, and my family was one of the families he delivered the newspapers to. One cold, wintery day he didn't deliver our paper, and my father called and asked his son to bring it. Fast forward years later to when that paperboy's father is my physics teacher, who somehow remembers that incident and associates my family name to it. He said something to the effect of, "So you're from that family that made us go out again to deliver a newspaper in the middle of a blizzard."

In my junior year, our English teacher was a recent graduate from Youngstown College (the name then). What I'm going to relate is something I wish we hadn't done. One day the whole class, me included, decided to boycott her class. Nobody would answer any of her questions. Quite regrettable.

A final memory from my high school days at Rayen. It was spring of 1964. There was a school assembly, and one of our classmates, Tim Jones, gave an unforgettable rendition of the song *Unchained Melody,* a song that a year later was an international success by the Righteous Brothers and was the theme song of the 1990 movie *Ghost.* Most people don't know it, but *Unchained Melody* was written to be the theme song of the 1955 prison movie *Unchained.* Hence the song title.

# CHAPTER 17

# FIRST JOB

In February of 1958, the number-one song was *Get a Job,* written and performed by a group called the Silhouettes. The song is about a guy whose wife or girlfriend wakes him up every morning, throwing the want ads at him and telling him to "get a job." The song had the memorable beginning:

*Yip yip yip yip yip yip yip*
*Sha na na na na, Sha na na na*

*Get a Job* was an example of doo-wop, a genre of rhythm and blues that originated in African-American communities in the 1940s and continued until the early 1960s. Doo-wop was performed by groups, included nonsense syllables, and had a simple beat with simple lyrics.

Over the years, I worked at a number of different jobs, which I'll comment on, but first here are some strange jobs you might (or might not) want to apply for: Paranormal Guide (leads tours through haunted homes and castles); Dog Food Taster (ensures the food is of high quality and taste); Human Scarecrow (sits in the middle of a cornfield and scares away birds).

The word "job" usually has the idea of "a regular remunerative position," but here I'll use it in the sense of "the work that you do to earn money."

My first job was helping a friend on his paper route. I was

twelve years old, so the year was 1959 or 1960. A paper route was the job of delivering newspapers to people's houses. This was a typical job for us "boomers" when we were kids. (Another typical job for kids at that time was to cut the grass on people's lawns.) My friend Mike Eisenstot paid me to deliver newspapers to the subscribers on some of the streets on his route.

The *Youngstown Vindicator* newspapers were delivered to street corners, and the paperboys folded them, put them in a large canvas shoulder bag, walked to the streets on their routes, and threw the papers onto the subscribers' porches. Then, once a month, the paperboys would go to their customers' houses and collect the payments. My paper route experience was short-lived: I lasted about two weeks.

Things have changed since then. Today my newspaper comes in a plastic bag, which the delivery person (no longer a boy's activity) throws onto the driveway. Back then, plastic bags weren't used. (The plastic bag was invented in 1965.) Plastic bags weren't even needed because newspapers were thrown onto porches.

Houses (at least in Youngstown) had front porches. People enjoyed sitting on the porches in the evening, just relaxing and chatting. Today, I suppose, if houses had porches (which here in Seattle they don't), people would sit next to each other, silently looking at their phones. A sad commentary on life today.

Around that time, I had a good friend, Jimmy Witt. Many an evening we would sit on his porch, a pitcher of his mother's iced tea on the table in front of us, playing board and card games (Canasta, Hearts, Go Fish), or just "shooting the breeze" (so to speak). What did we talk about? I don't remember, and if I did, I probably couldn't print it.

Sometimes we were on the porch during a raging thunderstorm. It wasn't scary or frightening; actually, it was quite relaxing. We felt safe on the porch (and we didn't know how dangerous lightning can be). A lightning bolt is five times hotter than the surface of the sun.

You're more likely to be struck by lightning than you are to win the lottery. The odds of getting struck by lightning are about 1 in 500,000. In contrast, the odds of winning the Powerball lottery on a single ticket are 1 in 292,000,000. Worldwide lightning kills around two thousand people a year, but strangely national park ranger Roy Sullivan (1912–1983) was never one of them. Why strangely? Because over a period of thirty-five years he was struck by lightning and survived, not once but an incredible seven times.

We always think these things never come close to home, never happen to someone we know, but sadly this wasn't the case. The year was 1969. My cousin Michael Chevlen (to me, he was Mikie) worked at Northside Hospital. He was an orderly (hospital assistant) in the emergency room. An ambulance brought someone who had been struck by lightning. Mikie was there to assist and was shocked to see that the dead person on the stretcher, a young kid, was a friend of his (Lee Malowitz) who had been struck by lightning on a golf course where he had been working as a caddy. This young kid was also the younger brother of one of my school classmates, Michael Malowitz.

# CHAPTER 18

# MORE FIRST JOBS

**During the ten years I lived in Youngstown** (1954–1964), I made several attempts to earn money besides my short-lived stint as a paperboy. I had four other little "jobs" between the ages of fourteen and sixteen.

We lived on Elm Street, not far from the Henry Stambaugh Golf Course on Gypsy Lane. I was a Boy Scout and wanted to buy a special scout hat, a hat with a stiff, wide brim and a four-corner peaked crown. When camping, the hat would protect me from the rain and the sun and could be used to fan the flames of a fire to get it going strong to produce white-hot coals for cooking.

So for a short time, I shagged balls on a driving range at the golf course, which meant that I ran after golf balls and brought them back to whoever had hit them. My shagging (in the sense of running after golf balls; there's also a slang sense, more British than American, meaning "to have sex") lasted about three weeks, just long enough to buy my hat.

Shagging balls was my only contact with golf; I had absolutely no interest in hitting a ball a long distance and then running after it. However, many of my uncles and cousins were avid golfers, which reminds me of a story about my cousin Jack Chevlen.

Around the time Jack was twelve, Uncle Harold had "The Talk" with him. "The Talk" is an expression meaning an awkward conversation between a teenager and their parents about sex and puberty. It's when preadolescents are told "the facts of life," are told about "the birds and the bees." Maybe it should be called "the lions and the rabbits." A male lion can mate up to fifty times in a single day, and a single European rabbit can produce 360 bunnies over the course of a year.

After Uncle Harold gave him "The Talk" and had explained that he wasn't brought by a stork, he asked Jack if he had any questions. Jack said, "Actually I do." Uncle Harold nervously awaited what was sure to be an awkward question. Jack's question: "Do you have any tips for my golf game?"

For a short time (two or three weeks), I sold magazines. I saw an ad in the paper, went to an office in a downtown building, and was given the job along with several other young kids around my age (fifteen).

We were driven to rural areas. Our job was to go up to houses and convince the adult who was at home (almost always a woman) to take a subscription to one of the magazines we were selling. Some popular magazines of the 1960s were *Life; Harper's Bazaar; Ladies Home Journal; Scientific American; Sports Illustrated; Time Magazine; Popular Mechanics;* and *The Saturday Evening Post.*

When someone answered the door, we would always begin our sales pitch with the question, "Do you have phone service?" In the early 1960s, most urban households had telephones, but phones were less common in the rural areas where we were selling our magazines. The line served as a lead-in to the sales pitch, but it also ruled out people who couldn't afford a magazine subscription.

During one or two summers, I worked at The Northside Swimming Pool. I worked in the men's changing room. They would come up to the counter, and I would give them a basket along with a card with the number corresponding to the basket. They would change into their swimsuits, put their clothes in the basket, and bring it back to me. It was a good summer job for a young kid. I wish I could say, "It couldn't have been better." But I can't say that. Like George Washington, I cannot tell a lie. Yes. It could've been better: if I had been working in the women's changing room!

And one final "job" in Youngstown. I was fifteen. I was walking down the street. Uncle Norman saw me, stopped, and asked where I was going. I told him I was going to go to some stores to see if I could get part-time work. He said, "Hop in. I have a friend who can probably use you." So, he took me to a carwash. It was arranged for me to start the next day. My job was to dry the cars as they came out from under the soapy sprays and the mechanical brushes. Once again, I cannot tell a lie. I only lasted one day!

This reminds me of my brother, who actually enjoys (yes, enjoys) washing the family cars. There are days when he happily (yes, happily) spends all morning washing his car and Mindy's car, as well as the cars of each of his three kids. As they say in Brazil. "Cada louco com sua mania" (every crackpot with his mania). Me? I never washed a car in my life. That's what car washes are for. (Or my brother, but alas, he didn't live nearby when I had my cars.)

# CHAPTER 19

# BOY SCOUTS: A LITTLE BACKGROUND

Aside from my family (immediate and extended), the Jewish Community Center, and a few good friends, the most important influence on my life while growing up in Youngstown was the Boy Scouts, an organization originally for boys ages eleven to sixteen that aims to develop in them moral character, patriotism, good citizenship, and kind behavior. There's also an emphasis on participation and skill in various outdoor activities, notably camping, hiking, backpacking, and woodcraft (practical knowledge of woods and forests).

These ideals are set out in the Scout Motto ("be prepared"), in the Scout Slogan ("do a good deed daily"), and in the Scout Oath ("On my honor, I will do my best to do my duty to God and my country and to obey the Scout Law; to help other people at all times; to keep myself physically strong, mentally awake, and morally straight").

And in the Scout Law (a scout is trustworthy, loyal, helpful, friendly, courteous, kind, obedient, cheerful, thrifty, brave, clean, and reverent). Nothing less than a saint!

There's a saying, "Once a Scout, always a Scout." (Actually, I never heard that; I just thought it would be a good lead-in to my next little story.) One day, when I was a senior in college at

UCLA, I found myself in a unique situation, a situation where I could do a good deed and at the same time fulfill five of the Scout Laws (be helpful, friendly, courteous, kind, and cheerful).

As I was about to enter Rolfe Hall, the building that houses the Department of Spanish and Portuguese, I noticed that behind me there was a cute, shapely girl. So, I went in and held the door open for her. Her response to my chivalrous gesture (which, of course, had no "second intentions") was one word uttered with a piercing look of disdain: "Chauvinist!" Oh well, at least I tried to do my good deed. But I wasn't deterred from continuing to do my daily good deed. Then and there I decided I would concentrate on helping old ladies cross the street, usually because they wanted to cross, but that wasn't a prerequisite.

The Boy Scout movement was founded by Robert Stephenson Smyth Baden-Powell (1857–1941), a British cavalry officer who had learned the forest lore and woodcraft ways of the American frontiersmen. Baden-Powell put this information into a small book, *Aids to Scouting* (meaning reconnaissance). Published in 1899, it was a military field manual that helped train the British soldiers fighting in the Second Boer War (1899–1902) in South Africa.

After the war, Baden-Powell decided to write a nonmilitary book for adolescents that, in addition to woodlore, would also emphasize patriotism, morality, and good deeds. The result was the 1908 book *Scouting for Boys*, which presented Scouting from the perspective of outdoorsmen (rather than military men) and added the Scout Oath and the Scout Law. The success of the new book led to the official founding of the Boy Scout movement, which by the end of 1908 had sixty thousand registered scouts.

The American version of the Boy Scouts had its origins in an event that (allegedly) occurred in London in 1909. Chicago publisher William Boyce was lost in the fog when a Boy Scout came to his aid. After guiding Boyce to his destination, the boy refused a tip, explaining that as a Boy Scout he couldn't accept payment for doing a good deed. This anonymous gesture inspired Boyce to organize a national US scouting organization, which was incorporated on February 8, 1910, as the Boy Scouts of America.

# CHAPTER 20

# I JOIN THE BOY SCOUTS

In March of 1959, I joined Boy Scout Troop 19, which was sponsored by Rodef Sholom Temple. I was eleven years old and in the sixth grade at Harding Elementary School. The troop met Thursday evenings from 7 to 8:30 in the Strouss Social Hall at Rodef Sholom Temple.

Probably the single best thing that ever happened to me. Well, being born would have to top that, and then there was meeting Neusa and the birth of our kids and grandchildren. But it would be safe to say Scouting was an extraordinary influence on my childhood. It gave me a sense of belonging, accomplishment, pride, and self-worth.

Boy Scout Troop 19 was founded in 1913 (at Temple Rodef Sholom). That means it was established within three years of the beginning of the Boy Scouts in the United States, putting it among the first troops in the nation.

Scouting depends on adult volunteers. Without them, there would be no Boy Scout troops. Their contributions to the lives of young boys cannot be overstated. They are "unsung heroes." The most important volunteer is the scoutmaster, the leader of the troop (which is divided into subgroups of around eight boys called patrols). The first scoutmaster of Troop 19 was Herbert R. Hartzell (1890–1962).

My first scoutmaster was Doctor William Gordon (1928–2022), who, when he wasn't drilling the Scout troop ("Attention," "Parade Rest") was drilling (and billing) his patients. He was a dentist (and retired from his dental practice at age 90!). Unfortunately, I never really knew him because he was the scoutmaster for only a short time.

By my calculations, he was around thirty-one years old. So young, and yet he was generously giving his time to the well-being of some twenty young kids when, after a long day of work, he could've been at home sitting on the sofa watching the hit TV shows of the late 1950s, such as *I Love Lucy; The Honeymooners; Perry Mason; The Twilight Zone; Dragnet; The Ed Sullivan Show; Gunsmoke; Wagon Train; I've Got a Secret; Have Gun Will Trave;* and *Bonanza.* And this on television sets with antennas called rabbit ears and sans remote control. Well, not exactly without. The remote control at that time was asking your son or daughter to go over to the television and change the channel for you.

The only scoutmaster I really remember is Doctor Seymour Feuer (1923–2004), who, like Doctor Gordon, was a dentist. He was my scoutmaster over a period of several years, until I left Youngstown in 1964, and was an especially important positive influence on my life.

Once the patrol leaders had a meeting with Doctor Feuer in his dental office to make plans for a camping trip (this was in 1961, and I was thirteen years old). Dickie Friedman and I decided to trade punches in the arm. We would hit each other in the arm as hard as we could, but since he was bigger than me (and about a year older), I got two punches for his one (two for one seemed like a good deal). This went on for about fifteen minutes, and all the while Doctor Feuer calmly conducted the meeting, not the least bit annoyed by our antics. Never once did he say, "Can you guys cut it out?"

The next day, Dickie didn't come to school (we were freshmen at Rayen High School). It turns out I had broken a blood vessel in his arm. After that, I could've told my friends to just call me "Ali," as in Muhammad Ali (1942–2016), the great American professional boxer and political activist. But this happened before Ali's famous 1964 heavyweight championship fight with Sonny "The Bear" Liston.

Before the fight, Ali (then known as Cassius Clay) proclaimed he would "float like a butterfly and sting like a bee" (and he did). He also penned a poem forecasting his victory:

> Clay comes out to meet Liston and Liston starts to retreat,
> If Liston goes back an inch farther he'll end up in a
> ringside seat.

> Clay swings with a left,
> Clay swings with a right,
> Just look at young Cassius carry the fight.

> Liston keeps backing, but there's not enough room,
> It's a matter of time until Clay lowers the boom.

> Then Clay lands with a right, what a beautiful swing,
> And the punch raised the bear clear out of the ring.

Some years afterward, Ali famously said, "It's hard to be humble when you're as great as I am." Ali's larger-than-life persona left an indelible mark on the world of sports and beyond (political activism and racial justice); not for nothing, he was included in Time Magazine's "The Most Influential People of the 20th Century."

# CHAPTER 21

# CAMP STAMBAUGH

**Beginning in July of 1959, every summer I would** spend a week with our troop at Camp Stambaugh, which opened in July of 1919 on land donated by the prominent local industrialist Henry H. Stambaugh (1858–1919). It's the second oldest continuously operating Scout camp in Ohio and is tied for the ninth oldest in the United States.

We checked in on a Sunday afternoon and checked out the following Saturday morning. As soon as we checked in, we went to our designated campsite, which had tents and a wooden enclosed two-seat latrine. The toilet seat was a wooden plank with two big holes. There was obviously some kind of shower facility in each campsite, but I don't remember anything about it. (Hello, Freud!)

We slept in sleeping bags on a metal-frame bed raised from the floor, two scouts to a tent. I don't remember who shared a tent with me, but once there was a guest who spent part of the night under one of our beds. This guest was masked, but I assure you it wasn't the Lone Ranger.

The Lone Ranger was a fictional masked frontiersman (on the 1950s television series of that name) who fought outlaws in the American Old West accompanied by his Native-American friend, Tonto, who called The Lone Ranger "Kimosabe," meaning "trusty friend."

Each episode opened with a part of Rossini's *William Tell Overture* (who can forget that iconic opening?) and ended (after the Lone Ranger had saved the day) with someone crying out "Who was that masked man?" and The Lone Ranger answering "Hi-Yo, Silver! Away!" I had always thought it was Hi Ho, but I was wrong.

Nor was the masked guest under the bed Zorro. Created by Johnston McCulley in 1919, Zorro was a dashing masked vigilante who defends the commoners and indigenous peoples of California against corrupt and tyrannical officials and other villains during the latter era of Mexican California (1821–1848). This was also a television series from 1957–1959 starring Guy Williams (1924–1989).

No, the masked guest was a racoon. We had placed some food under our beds hoping to attract a racoon. We were half asleep (after having spent about two hours telling the kind of jokes only twelve-year-old boys think are funny) when we heard something scratching and chewing under the bed. Then it stopped as suddenly as it had begun. The next morning, the food was gone. And luckily it was a racoon and not a skunk.

We didn't have to cook (but we did have to do KP—kitchen clean-up). Meals were in a dining hall, which (thanks to a donation in 1955 from my uncles' company, Century Foods) had an eight-foot cooler. Food was prepared by the camp staff. I don't remember what we ate, but lunch and dinner always had some kind of juice, which we called "bug juice."

Days were spent doing various scoutcraft activities (identifying the local trees, trying to spot animals, tying knots, canoeing, swimming in a lake, working on Second and First-

Class Scoutcraft requirements). There was an area to practice skills using a compass. You were given a card with sets of compass directions and steps to pace off in order to arrive at a predetermined location.

There was an obstacle course you tried to complete as fast as you could. There were ten car tires lying on the ground. You had to step in each of them. There was a wall you had to climb over. There was something you had to crawl under (don't remember what it was). There was a rope hanging from a tree branch that you had to climb. It wasn't exactly US Marines level, but it was a good physical workout.

There was a crafts room where you could do woodcarving, perhaps making a slide (a device to fasten the scout neckerchief in front of your chest). Other activities included basket weaving and lanyard braiding.

Every evening, around 5 p.m., there was an inspection of the troop's campsite. Everything was expected to be impeccable. It was a contest to see which troop got the highest score. Any infringement meant points deducted. We stood rigid, perfectly still, "at attention," in front of our tents while someone from the camp staff performed the inspection. If we failed to hold a straight face, points were deducted. Our uniforms were expected to be in perfect order—clean, no button unbuttoned, nothing out of place. Shirts tucked in. Neckerchiefs carefully arranged around the neck. Beds made; all equipment properly stored. The tent as orderly and as neat as your mother wished you kept your room at home. Note: I said, "wished."

Wednesday evening was an all-camp campfire event (other days, troops had their individual evening campfires). Parents were invited. It took place in a special amphitheater with bleachers. We sang songs, and each troop performed a skit. Here are some songs we sang: *John Jacob Jingleheimer Schmidt; Do Your Ears Hang Low?; If You're Happy and You Know It; On Top of Old Spaghetti;* and *The Ants Go Marching One by One.*

The evening ended (as did all of our evening campfires) with all of the Scouts singing the taps lyrics:

Day is done, gone the sun,
From the lake, from the hills, from the sky;
All is well, safely rest,
God is nigh.

These short lines, with their haunting and poignant melody, always left us with a feeling of calm, serenity, and peace. They signaled the end of the day and bedtime (with pleasant dreams).

Camp Stambaugh was great fun. I enjoyed every minute of it. Well, almost every minute. I didn't enjoy KP or latrine duty. Mark Twain said, "Make it a point to do something every day that you don't want to do." Good advice. I'll try to follow it in my next incarnation.

# CHAPTER 22

# TENDERFOOT TO FIRST CLASS

**A Boy Scout troop is made up of smaller units** of around eight Scouts called patrols, each one with a designated leader responsible for planning activities (for example, hikes, camping trips, and community service activities) and for guiding the members towards reaching their Scouting goals.

My first patrol leader was Eddie Friedman. We would meet at his house, and he would instruct us on the requirements for Tenderfoot, the first rank in the Scouting movement (which is followed by Second Class, First Class, Star, Life, and Eagle). He was eighteen at the time and getting ready to go to college, so he wasn't my patrol leader for a long time. I don't remember Eddie well, but I do remember hero-worshiping him. He was the first older scout influence on my life, if only for a period of a few months.

My first Scouting friends included Steve Solomon, Fred Dumas, Dickie Friedman (Eddie's brother), Marshal Wexler, and Bobby Braitman. Bobby reminded me of Alfred E. Newman.

So who is Alfred E. Newman? Alfred E. Newman is the fictitious mascot and cover boy of the American humor magazine *Mad*, a magazine founded in 1952 and noted for its witty satire on all aspects of popular culture, politics, entertainment, and public figures. Alfred E. Newman, with his gap-tooth smile, freckles, red hair, big nose, protruding ears (and his "What, me worry?" motto), appeared on the cover of each issue.

*Mad* was one of my two favorite magazines when I was growing up. The other? Did you really think the other magazine was *Playboy?* What kind of a Boy Scout do you think I was? My other favorite was the Scouting magazine *Boys' Life*. Okay, so *Playboy* was my favorite, at a slightly older age. Great articles and interviews, you know.

Between 1959 and 1960, I went on to earn the next two ranks in Scouting (Second Class and First Class). My patrol leader was Billy Weimer, who was about two years older than me. One of the requirements for First Class was the ability to (safely) use an ax. I remember learning to cut wood with an ax in back of his house. I was small for my age and could hardly hold the ax in my hand, but somehow I managed to cut some wood that day (and not lose a finger in the process).

At any rate, Lizzie Borden I was not. In 1892 Lizzie Borden of Fall River, Massachusetts, was accused, tried, and acquitted of killing her father and stepmother with an ax, giving rise to the folk rhyme:

Lizzie Borden took an ax.
and gave her mother forty whacks.
When she saw what she had done,
she gave her father forty-one.

Another requirement for my First-Class badge was to draw a map that someone unfamiliar with a camp location could use to find their way to the camp. I made a map from my house on Elm Street to the Strouss family estate, where we

Scouts would often spend a day exploring the woods behind the estate house.

To get to the woods, we had to cross a field that was behind the stable, which itself was behind the main house. So the first stop was to the stable to pat the horses on the head. A day in the woods on the Strouss estate, making a fire and cooking our lunch (which we always thought was delicious, but we were young and not very discerning) was a young Scout's paradise.

I made my map and presented it to Billy. He studied it, thought for a moment, signed my requirement card, wrote something on the map, and gave it back to me. Was the comment going to be praise for my work? Was he going to say it was one of the best maps he had ever seen? It turns out the comment was a succinct piece of advice: "Learn to spell!"

# CHAPTER 23

# PATROL LEADER

**Around the end of 1961, I became a patrol leader.** Our patrol was named "The Frontiersmen." I don't remember why we chose that name. Maybe we were inspired by Walt Disney's TV miniseries (1954–1955) about the legendary American folk hero and frontiersman Davy Crockett (1786–1836), who died in the Battle of the Alamo (the most famous battle in Texas's fight for independence from Mexico).

We "boomers" grew up with the TV image of Davy Crocket, portrayed by Fess Parker (1924–2010) with his coonskin cap (a hat made from the skin and fur of a raccoon), and we all knew the words to the show's theme song, *The Ballad of Davy Crocket.*

> Born on a mountain top in Tennessee,
> Greenest state in the land of the free.
> Raised in the woods so's he knew ev'ry tree.
> Kilt him a b'ar when he was only three.
> Davy, Davy Crockett, king of the wild frontier!

I went on many hikes with my patrol or just with one or two fellow Scouts. One of those hikes was in 1961. Lenny Rome and I (age thirteen) left my house on Elm Street on a chilly April morning at 8 a.m. Our destination was Mill Creek Park, a large metropolitan park, about five miles from my house.

We didn't know how to get to the park. I took out a map from the back of the phone book (back then, every house received a big book that listed the names, addresses, and phone numbers of everyone who had a phone). At first we went a few blocks in the wrong direction: I was pointing the north end of the map south (anyone who knows me won't be surprised).

We finally arrived at the park. From my account of the hike: "We came to a place to eat and built a fire. At first it didn't look like much of a fire, but it left nice coals. I had a hamburger smothered in potatoes and a baked apple. Lenny had soup, potato sticks, and carrots. We put out the fire, visited the Old Mill, and returned home."

Mill Creek Park brings back another memory: Lindley Vickers (1900–1981). Lindley, or Mr. Vickers as I thought of him, was the park's naturalist. Not to be confused with a "naturist," someone who practices nudism. Maybe he was a naturist-naturalist, but when I met him, I'm sure he was wearing clothes.

Mr. Vickers had a daily column ("A Nature Diary") in the *Youngstown Vindicator* in which he described his nature observations. This brings to mind Henry David Thoreau's 1854 book, *Walden, or Life in the Woods*. Maybe Mr. Vickers was Thoreau reincarnated. During all the years I lived in Youngstown (1954–1964), his column was the first thing I read in the newspaper.

# CHAPTER 24

# ON TO EAGLE

In September of 1961 (age thirteen), I achieved the rank of Star, and in February of 1962 (age fourteen), the rank of Life. In February of 1963 (age fifteen), I obtained the rank of Eagle, the highest rank in Scouting. I was actually the 1,000th Eagle Scout in the Mahoning Valley Council. Other Eagle Scouts from troop 19 before me were Steven Birenbaum, Alan Witchner, Billie Weimer, and Shelly Harr.

To obtain the rank of Eagle, a Scout must have been a Life Scout for at least six months, earned a minimum of twenty-one merit badges, fourteen of which are mandatory, demonstrated exemplary Scout spirit (following the Scout Oath and Law), demonstrated leadership within their troop, and (as of 1965) planned and executed a major service project. I actually went a little beyond and a year later earned a Bronze Palm, an award for earning an additional five merit badges after receiving the Eagle award.

The first Eagle Scout medal in the United States was awarded in 1912 to Arthur Rose Eldred (1895–1951). Here are some famous (and one infamous) Eagle Scouts: Gerald Ford (US President); Harrison Ford (actor); Martin Luther King Jr. (civil rights leader); Michael Jordan (basketball player); Neil Armstrong (first man on the moon); Sam Walton (founder of

Walmart); Steven Spielberg (filmmaker); Guion Bluford (first African-American in space); and Charles Whitman (University of Texas tower sniper killer).

As I said, to achieve the rank of Eagle, you have to have earned at least twenty-one merit badges, which are awards based on meeting requirements within an area of study. The merit badge is a circular patch with an image representing the badge's topic. Merit badges are displayed on a sash, which can be worn with the Boy Scout uniform on formal occasions. I earned a total of twenty-six merit badges. Here are the ones I have a record of:

> Animal Husbandry; Basketry; Camping; Citizenship in the Community; Citizenship in the Home; Citizenship in the Nation; Cooking; Fingerprinting; Firemanship; First Aid; Forestry; Hiking; Life Saving; Nature; Personal Fitness; Pioneering; Public Health; Scholarship; Soil and Water Conservation; Swimming; Wood Carving; and World Brotherhood.

As I look back at the merit badges I earned, I can't help but wonder and, in some cases, be amused. I mean, seriously? "Animal Husbandry" (I had to describe how hogs are made profitable); "Basketry" (I had to plan and weave a large basket). When I was in college at UCLA, we used to joke, saying, "What are you majoring in, basket weaving?"

And "Fingerprinting" (I had to take a clear and legible set of fingerprints). Maybe I should've been an FBI agent instead of a teacher. Actually, fingerprinting is a useful skill to have. I mean, then you can always identify who stole the cookie from the cookie jar.

# CHAPTER 25

# OTHER AWARDS AND ACHIEVEMENTS

In 1962, I was inducted into the Order of the Arrow (OA), an honor society composed of Scouts and Scouters (adult members of the Boy Scouts) who, elected by their peers, best exemplify the Scout Oath and Law in their daily lives. Inducted members are organized into local lodges that foster fellowship, promote camping, and render service to Boy Scout councils and their communities.

The induction took place on an overnight camp at Camp Stambaugh. Each inductee had to find his own place to sleep and make his own shelter (no tents were provided). But the hardest part for me was that we had to go silent, not utter a single word, for twenty-four hours. That same year, I was elected secretary of our lodge, Neatoka Lodge 396.

In February of 1963, I was awarded the Ner Tamid, the Jewish Scout religious award. In the summer of that year (age fifteen), I was senior patrol leader of our troop at Camp Stambaugh. I was in charge of our troop during our week at camp and was expected to plan activities and guide the other scouts throughout the week. At the end of their week at camp, the senior patrol leaders are awarded the Stambaugh Medal.

In 1964, our troop had a merit badge show in the Strouss

Social Hall of our temple. Each participant made an exhibit relative to one or more of the merit badges he had earned. Kind of like a middle school science fair, but for merit badges. I spent four months preparing my exhibit about camping. I made over seventy miniatures of many aspects of camping (fires, shelter, cooking, etc.). I even built a full-size pine-bough shelter. My exhibit completely filled the stage. I won first prize and was awarded a rather large trophy.

In February of 1964, at a Scout Sabbath (a yearly religious ceremony meant to mark the February 8th founding of the Boy Scouts in the United States in 1910), I received the Lee Harold Garson trophy as Troop 19's "Outstanding Scout of the Year."

Lee Harold Garson was a former Scout in Troop 19 who had been killed in action in World War Two. His mother established the award in her son's memory. The "Garson" award was much coveted; it was like the Troop 19 Scouting Oscar. I wish I had thought to talk with Lee Harold's mother, to learn his story, to hear about his life. But, alas, I was sixteen, and the thought never occurred to me.

# CHAPTER 26

# PHILMONT

In August of 1962 (age fourteen), along with another thirty-three Scouts and four adult leaders, I went to Philmont National Boy Scout Ranch (located in a subrange of the Rocky Mountains) for ten days of hiking and camping in the rugged northern New Mexico wilderness. And rugged it was. Mountainous terrain, deep valleys, and forest-covered slopes. Fast-moving creeks and streams. (Ever try crossing a stream with a heavy backpack by walking on a log, all the time trying not to lose your balance?)

We went by a chartered air-conditioned bus with a bathroom at the back. It was a four-day trip from Youngstown to Cimarron, the village in New Mexico a short distance from Philmont's headquarters. But there was nothing boring about the long days on the bus. We were constantly joking with our seatmates and then changing places with someone to continue talking and joking with someone else.

In the evening of the day we arrived, there was a campfire for all of the groups that had arrived from across the country. As each group introduced itself, saying where it was from, the group was silently classified as "Northerners" or "Southerners." When a troop announced itself, all the troops from that sector (North or South) gave rousing cheers. It was as if the Civil War

(1861–1865) had never ended.

Along with the traditional campfire songs, there was a cracker-eating contest: who could eat the most crackers in two minutes? One representative from each troop against someone who represented the Philmont staff. The staffer easily won because the challengers had been given crackers with peanut butter on them. The campfire that night ended with everyone singing the Philmont hymn, a beautiful song that captures the beauty of Philmont.

> Silver on the sage,
> Starlit skies above,
> Aspen covered hills,
> Country that I love.
>
> Philmont, here's to thee,
> Scouting Paradise,
> Out in God's country, tonight.
>
> Wind in whispering pines,
> Eagles soaring high,
> Purple mountains rise,
> Against an azure sky.
>
> Philmont, here's to thee,
> Scouting Paradise,
> Out in God's country tonight.

One particular day hike stands out in my memory. It was from our base camp to Trail Peak, which at 10,250 feet is the 9th highest peak in Philmont. Trail Peak is one of Philmont's most popular day-hike itineraries because at the top, there is the wreckage of a B-24d Liberator bomber that crashed into the summit in 1942 while on a training flight. Parts of the wing and other parts were still on the peak or in the surrounding area. The view from the summit was impressive: tree-covered slopes as far as you could see.

Before leaving, I bought a red wool Philmont jacket with a black felt bull on the upper left shoulder. I wore that jacket all the time, even five years later (1967), when I was studying at UCLA. That was my pseudo-hippie phase, so I wore the jacket draped over my shoulders like a cape. (Practicing for Hollywood to cast me as Batman? Dracula? Alas, Hollywood passed me over and cast Tom Cruise as Lestat in the 1994 film *Interview with the Vampire.*)

# CHAPTER 27

# JAMBOREE

In 1964, I attended the Sixth National Scout Jamboree held from July 17–23 at Valley Forge, Pennsylvania. The national jamboree is usually held every four years and is attended by thousands of Scouts from all over the nation and (in smaller numbers) from around the world. The first national jamboree was held in 1937 and attracted 25,000 Scouts. In 1964, there were around 51,000 attendees.

Each unit is assigned to a campsite. We would walk around the sprawling campgrounds, visiting other campsites, with our collection of patches and neckerchiefs in tow. We would sit on the floor in the tent of a Scout from another state or country and have a trading session. We would spread out our collection of patches, neckerchiefs, and slides. There would be offers and counter-offers. Either a deal was reached, or we just chatted and parted ways, looking for someone else to trade with.

The president of the United States, Lyndon Johnson (1908–1973), spoke at the closing ceremony. At the time, all I knew was that the president of the United States was addressing us. Only years later did I realize what a great president he had been (despite his notorious crudeness).

Johnson was unbelievably crude. He liked to lean over people, spitting, swearing, belching, or laughing in their faces.

Once he even relieved himself on a secret serviceman who was shielding him from public view. When the man looked horrified, Johnson simply said, "That's all right, son. It's my prerogative." Or he would drag people into the bathroom with him—forcing them to continue their conversations with him as he used the toilet (unbelievable, but true).

However, his crudeness aside, Johnson had transformative domestic programs (his "Great Society"). Johnson's legacy includes the Civil Rights Act of 1964, which prohibited racial discrimination, and in 1965, Medicare, a health insurance program for elderly Americans (thank you, Lyndon). But those achievements were overshadowed by the Vietnam War. Anti-war protests sprang up on college campuses and in major cities (I participated, chanting, "Hell, no. We won't go").

By 1968, more than 500,000 US troops were in Vietnam, and there seemed to be no end in sight. Then on Sunday, March 31, 1968, President Johnson shocked the nation, but it wasn't by a crude remark or act. I was sitting in the TV room of Rieber Hall (my student residence hall at UCLA) watching *Rowan & Martin's Laugh-In* (a show that was characterized by rapid-fire gags and sketches, many of which were politically charged or contained sexual innuendos).

To our dismay, the show was interrupted by a special announcement by the president of the United States (what could he have to say that was more important than *Laugh-In*?). Johnson announced he wouldn't be running for reelection in the 1968 presidential election. The room erupted in applause and cheers. Because of the war, he was unpopular with college students who dreaded the thought of being drafted and sent to fight in Vietnam.

But in 1964, there was no talk about the war, which was

just beginning. All I knew was the president was speaking. He said the United States was founded on the recognition that "all men were equal in the eyes of God." And it would be up to us Scouts "to carry this idea forward. For it is not yet a reality for all in this land." He then urged us to be faithful to our Boy Scout oath, telling us our lives and the life of our country "will be the richer for it."

The night ended with a candlelight ceremony. All lights were extinguished. Total darkness. Each of us, all 51,000 of us, had been given a candle, which we then lit. The evening ended in a sea of candle flames. It was a solemn and unforgettable ending for what had been one of the most memorable events in my Scouting life.

CHAPTER 28

# JOHN WOLBOLDT

**Besides my scoutmaster (Dr. Seymour Feuer),** there was another unsung adult Scout hero in my life: John Wolboldt (1923–2014). John wasn't affiliated with my troop; he was scoutmaster of Troop 25 in Canfield, Ohio, a city/suburb about eight miles southwest of Youngstown.

I met John in the summer of 1961. I was at the yearly troop summer camp at Camp Stambaugh. Troop 25 had also chosen to be there that week. It was a happy coincidence; otherwise, I never would have met this unsung hero who contributed so much to my young adolescent life.

They say adolescence is a difficult time and that adolescents make life difficult for their parents (and everyone around them). In Brazil, adolescents are jokingly called "aborrecentes," combining "aborrecer" (to annoy) with "adolescentes" (adolecents), giving a word meaning "adolescents who are annoying and exasperating." I don't remember having a difficult adolescence or being an "aborrescente." I was well-behaved (Scout's honor!). Maybe one of the reasons I was an "easy" adolescent was because I had unsung heroes like Dr. Feuer and John Wolboldt in my life.

Here's how I met John. I was looking for an adult to supervise my cooking merit badge. Someone suggested I go to

Troop 25's campsite and speak with John Wolboldt, which I did, and he accepted.

For the cooking merit badge, I had to cook a meal for John and his family (his wife and two sons). John lived in a somewhat rural area in Canfield and had a large woods behind his house. Perfect for what I needed to do. Here's the cooking merit badge requirement from 1961 (slightly abridged).

> Build a fire; (b) cook a satisfactory meal for at least four persons, including meat or fish, two fresh vegetables, and a desert that requires cooking, timing the cooking so that the courses will be ready to serve at the proper time; and (c) dispose of the garbage in a proper way, clean the utensils, put out the fire, and clean up the site thoroughly.

Anyone familiar with my cooking skills today (or lack of them) would probably say I should return the cooking merit badge or give it to my son Sérgio, who loves to grill meat and fish.

I don't remember how it started, but there were times when I would call John in the evening to discuss Scouting and other things in my life. I was around fourteen at the time. He took the time to listen to me. We would talk for about fifteen minutes. What a difference it made to a young fourteen-year-old boy! Not that I didn't have my parents to talk to. I did. But he was in Scouting, and we could talk about Scouting as well as other things.

John was one of the most recognized Scouters in Ohio. In 2012, at the age of eighty-nine, he was the oldest living Eagle Scout in the state and had been scoutmaster or assistant scoutmaster for over forty years. Now that's dedication!

But John almost never became a Scout. He hadn't really thought about joining the Boy Scouts until a life-changing event occurred when he was ten. He fell into the water at a church function, and a Boy Scout jumped in and saved his life. After that, he couldn't wait to be old enough to join. That Scout didn't only save John's life. That Scout indirectly influenced every boy who was lucky enough to be in Scouting with John Wolboldt.

# CHAPTER 29

# ALAN WITCHNER

Alan Witchner (1946–1970) was a little over a year older than me. We met when I joined the Boy Scouts. We became friends and often did things together at each other's house. Along with Jimmy Witt, Alan was my closest friend.

One of my favorite memories is of a time at his house. This would've been around 1960. Alan's mother made us a batch of home-made French fries. I have a mental picture of her deep-frying the potatoes, hearing them sizzle and crackle in the oil, and the smell of them as she served us the crisp fries.

This memory also has us listening to a kooky song on the radio. I think the song might have been *Wooly Bully* (recorded by Sam the Sham and the Pharaohs, who wore turbans and dressed in long Arabian robes). Some other kooky songs we listened to were *Does your Chewing Gum Lose its Flavor on the Bedpost Overnight?* (can't get kookier than that!); *Itsy Bitsy Teenie Weenie Yellow Polkadot Bikini; The Purple People Eater;* and *Witch Doctor,* which had the memorable lines "Ooo Eee, Ooo Ah Ah—Ting Tang Walla Walla Bing Bang."

Alan held all the leadership positions in the troop. He was a patrol leader, a senior patrol leader, a junior assistant scoutmaster, and an assistant scoutmaster. He was a member of the Knights of Dunamis, an honor society of Eagle Scouts. In

1963, I also joined the Knights and would go with him to Courts of Honor, where we would preside over the ceremony in which a Scout was being bestowed the Eagle award.

After Alan graduated from high school in 1964, he went to Carnegie Mellon University, where he was on the debate team, was active with a local Scout troop, and was in the ROTC (Reserve Officer Training Corps), a program run by the US military to train college students in military leadership. After he graduated, he was a First Lieutenant in the Air Force, stationed in Laredo, Texas, where he learned to fly jets and became a pilot-instructor, flying in a T-38 Talon, a high-altitude, supersonic jet trainer.

Sadly, Alan passed away suddenly on October 15, 1970, at the age of twenty-four. He had flown in the morning and in the afternoon was on a track running when he collapsed from cardiac arrhythmia. I was living in my UCLA off-campus apartment when my mother called to give me the news. I was shocked. I picked up the phone and called his parents—the most heavy-hearted phone call I have ever made.

My sister also knew Alan. She was having dinner with Uncle Norman's family when someone commented how sad it was that Alan Witchner had died so suddenly and so young. Maureen jumped up from the table and ran out of the room, sobbing hysterically.

Alan was loved and esteemed by everyone who knew him. A great loss for his family and his many friends. A great loss for Scouting because he surely would have become a scoutmaster. And he certainly would've been an unsung Scouting hero, an inspiration to countless youths.

# CHAPTER 30

# GROWING UP JEWISH: A LITTLE BACKGROUND

**Let me begin by stating I'm not religious. I'm not** a practicing Jew. I don't belong to, nor do I attend a synagogue. That being said, I'm proud of my Jewish cultural heritage. My contact with Judaism as a religion and as a culture was from 1954 to 1964 (ages eight to sixteen), when my family was living in Youngstown, Ohio. At the time, there was a sizable Jewish community. As a child growing up in a Jewish household, you couldn't help but absorb and be influenced by Jewish religion and culture.

There are three main branches of Judaism: Orthodox, Conservative, and Reform. Each one has its own practices according to how it understands and observes the Jewish religious laws.

Orthodox Judaism adheres to the strict observance of traditional Jewish law and rituals. One of the hallmarks of Orthodox Judaism is "keeping kosher," that is, eating food prepared according to Jewish law. Only certain kinds of food are permitted to be eaten (pork isn't, so no ham sandwiches); meat may not be eaten in the same meal with dairy products; animals whose meat may be eaten must be slaughtered in a prescribed fashion.

Another hallmark is the strict observance of Shabbat, the Jewish Sabbath, a day of rest and prayer that begins Friday evening when the sun goes down and ends Saturday evening after sunset. In the Torah (the first five books of the Hebrew Bible), there are many activities that are prohibited during Shabbat. Orthodox Jews interpret these prohibitions such that any activity that would interfere with the *spirit* of Shabbat is prohibited. Thus driving, buying, selling, working, writing, and even using electricity are prohibited.

Reform Judaism, which originated in Germany in 1809, emphasizes the Jewish ethical tradition over the strict observance of traditional biblical Jewish law. It incorporates choir and organ music into the service and doesn't observe strict dietary laws (keeping kosher) or the restriction of normal activities on the Sabbath.

Conservative Judaism represents a midpoint between Orthodox and Reform Judaism, adopting certain innovations such as driving to the synagogue (but nowhere else) on Shabbat but maintaining the traditional line on other matters, like keeping kosher. My aunts and uncles in Youngstown were Conservative Jews.

My family, however, practiced Reform Judaism. We belonged to the Rodef Sholom congregation, which me and some of my friends, being normal teenage wisecrackers, nicknamed "Roll'em & Choke'em." Rodef Sholom, which means Pursuers of Peace, was founded by German immigrants in 1867, and its first services were conducted in German. In 1915, a beautiful new temple of limestone and gray brick in a Moorish design was built on Elm Street across from Wick Park.

In the rear of the temple there were classrooms where

every Sunday I would attend classes to learn Hebrew and to learn about Jewish history and customs. I wasn't exactly a stellar student. Here are my grades for the sixth grade: Jewish history (B); Hebrew (C); customs and ceremonies (D). On my report card, my Sunday school teacher wrote, "Stephen is quiet and attentive. However, some of his work shows very little effort."

The rabbi was Sidney Berkowitz (1911–1983), who led the congregation from 1946 until his death. The cantor (a man who leads the prayers and songs in a Jewish religious service) was Lawrence Ehrlich (1917–2003), a rotund man renowned for his operatic voice, a melodious voice that I still remember. (I also remember he had a pretty daughter, Harriet.)

# CHAPTER 31

# BAR MITZVAH

**In January of 1961, I celebrated my bar mitzvah,** a religious coming-of-age ritual when a Jewish boy reaches the age of thirteen (there's a similar ceremony for a girl called a bat mitzvah). In part of the ceremony, the celebrant reads a portion from the Torah, which is written in Hebrew.

When the day for my bar mitzvah came, I was ready, and I don't remember being nervous. I had outsourced my nervousness to my sister. It was her job to be nervous for me. So she sat in the front row, giggling, nervous for both of us.

But I almost didn't have to outsource my nervousness: I almost didn't have a bar mitzvah. A few days before my bar mitzvah, the temple called my parents to tell them that they needed to pay the temple dues, which were in arrears; without that payment there would be no bar mitzvah. My family was always short on money and didn't have any way of making that payment. Aunt Helen (my mother's sister) and Uncle Harold to the rescue. They made the payment, and thanks to them, I had my bar mitzvah.

Bar mitzvahs at Temple Rodef Sholom were on Friday evenings. After a bar mitzvah, the congregation was invited to go downstairs to the Strouss Memorial Social Hall for refreshments offered by the family of the celebrant. There were always several long tables with bowls of punch and an assortment of pastries.

As part of our religious training, we were required to attend two and later three Friday services a month. We always hoped there would be a bar mitzvah because that meant there would be a reception afterwards. We always looked forward to the reception.

For me, the reception was the second-best thing about a bar mitzvah. The best thing? The bar mitzvah party. A week or two after the bar mitzvah, the celebrant's family hosted a party in a rented hall. There was always a buffet dinner, a disc jockey who played records with the latest hits, and dancing.

The big dance craze of the early sixties was *The Twist,* a song and dance made famous by Chubby Checker. My cousin Sandi Super actually won a twist contest while she was pregnant. She went into labor, and the next day her daughter, Pam, was born. So now you know. If you're pregnant and want to speed along the process, ask your smart speaker to play Chubby Checker and twist away. Other dance crazes of the 60s include *The Pony, The Jerk, The Mashed Potato, The Monster Mash, The Loco-motion,* and *The Watisi.*

I enjoyed the bar mitzvah parties. I enjoyed getting dressed up in a suit, putting on English Leather cologne, and chatting and joking with my friends. I didn't dance much at the parties for two reasons. First, between the ages of twelve and fifteen, I wasn't interested in girls. I chatted with girls in my classes, but there was never a "romantic" interest. The second reason I hardly ever danced was I was too busy eating.

I had actually forgotten how much I ate until I read my cousin Gary Aron's story written for an Aron family reunion.

He pondered if there was anything that could compare with our cousin Dana's wedding and all the wonderful desserts made by her brother, Brad, who's a first-rate chief, and concluded:

> Well. Actually, there was one thing. It was the amount of food Steven consumed at a Sunday brunch at Lake Merced Country Club. You know how country clubs have a plaque outside the locker room listing the golfers who have had holes-in-one. Well, at Lake Merced Country Club, there is a plaque in the kitchen honoring Steven.

Today I'm a moderate eater. When we eat out at a restaurant, I usually only eat about half of the food on my plate and ask for a box to take the rest home for my lunch the following day. Asking for a take-home box is the norm today. But when I was growing up, it wasn't common, so we would ask for a "doggie bag" as if we were taking the remaining food home for our pet dog.

# CHAPTER 32

# I AM A FOUNTAIN PEN

A traditional gift for a bar mitzvah boy was a fountain pen, a writing instrument that uses a pointed metal tip to deliver ink to the paper from an internal reservoir. There's a joke that at his bar mitzvah, a boy is so excited about the prospect of getting fountain pens that when he goes to give his "today I am a man" speech, he accidentally says, "Today I am a fountain pen."

I never said, "Today, I am a fountain pen," but I did receive quite a few. And a week or two after my bar mitzvah party, I remember grudgingly sitting down and writing thank-you notes. While writing a bar mitzvah thank-you note is a tedious task, learning to express thanks is one of the most important lessons a parent can teach a child. No child will wake up and spontaneously say, "I can't wait to get started writing the thank-you notes for my bar mitzvah presents."

As I look back over the years, I see that I could've done a better job of expressing my thanks. I did thank Maureen and Joel (my sister and brother-in-law) for everything they did for my kids. If it wasn't for them, my kids wouldn't have been able to come and live in the States. And on my uncle Norman's 90th birthday celebration, I thanked him for everything he did for us.

Yet, there are a number of people no longer here who I wish I could thank. Tell them how much I appreciate what they did for me. Maybe I did thank them. I'm not sure. But they deserved a "special thanks." I should've written them a letter expressing my thanks. I should've sent them a thank-you card, a physical card, not an ecard from 123greetings.com (which didn't even exist back then).

I present this, not so much as a few regrets (and who doesn't have some regrets?), but more as a little "boomer wisdom." Benjamin Franklin (1706–1790) once said, "Life's tragedy is that we get old too soon and wise too late." Now that I'm a little older and a lot wiser (or is it a lot older and a little wiser?), I tell my kids that their birthday present will be a half hour of my "fatherly advice." Look, it might do them some good, and even if it doesn't, it saves me some money. So here are a few of those "departed" I wish I could thank.

- Professor Ruy Alencar, for bringing me to Brazil and for his constant support.

- Moysés Israel, a Jewish businessman and civic leader in Manaus who supported several of my projects while I was a teacher at the Federal University of Amazonas.

- Aunt Mary, for a gift that made a big difference in my life. You'll meet her in Part Six, story 73.

- Dr. Seymore Feuer and John Wolboldt, who you met when I talked about my time in the Boy Scouts.

Aunt Helen and Uncle Harold deserve a special mention. As I said, if it wasn't for Aunt Helen and Uncle Harold, I wouldn't have had my bar mitzvah. They were always there for my family. When my parents had to travel to nearby cities for their nightclub performances, it was in Aunt Helen and Uncle Harold's car.

Uncle Harold was the family doctor for the extended Aron family of aunts, uncles, and cousins. Once, when I was sick, Uncle Harold came to the house. That was a bygone time in the past when a doctor would come to your house in the middle of the night. I was eight years old, had an earache, and had been crying.

Little did I know I was soon going to have another reason to cry. Uncle Harold had me stick out my tongue and say "AHHHH," peered into my mouth and ear, opened his black doctor's bag, took out a syringe and a vial of penicillin, and gave me a shot in my "tuchus," my "tushi." I could've said in my "rear end," but I thought it would be more appropriate to use the Yiddish terms, which is how my parents referred to this part of the body. I don't remember turning to Uncle Harold and saying, "Thanks. I appreciate that shot!"

Well, maybe I'll do better in my next incarnation, that is, if I don't come back as a Bladderwort (a carnivorous plant that traps small aquatic animals in its bladder), a Pink Fairy Armadillo (has a pink bony armor shell), a Spanish Dancer (a sea-slug that swims like it's doing a flamenco dance), a Thorny Devil (an Australian lizard covered in spikes and scales), or an eagle (which according to a silly Facebook quiz is my destiny).

# CHAPTER 33

# JEWISH COMMUNITY CENTER

**They say we should count our blessings. Who** are the "they"? Well, one of them was William Penn (1644–1718), founder of Pennsylvania), who said, "The secret of happiness is to count your blessings while others are adding up their troubles." Good advice, but I wonder what Penn's twelve slaves thought about this (apparently, he didn't ask them for their opinion).

One of my blessings while growing up in Youngstown was the Jewish Community Center (JCC), which offered social, cultural, and recreational programs in a Jewish environment. The JCC was founded in 1937, and the facility on Gypsy Lane opened in August of 1954. Thus it was in its infancy when I took part in the various activities that it offered.

There were two ways of getting to the Center. One way was to walk up Gypsy Lane and go in through the front of the building. The other was to walk up Granada Avenue and go in through the back. The only problem with going in through the back was that you had to go on a dirt path between two cemeteries (Anshe Emeth and Children of Israel), which were located behind the Center.

It wasn't much of a problem though, because I don't remember ever feeling spooked, even when I went home at dusk. Even in twilight, the graves didn't seem eerie. Maybe if I had traversed the cemetery at midnight under a full moon, my memories would've been different. But then what could I possibly be doing in a cemetery at midnight? I wasn't a "body snatcher" like the infamous William Burke, who in 1828 killed sixteen people and sold their corpses to a Scottish anatomist who used them for dissection during his lectures.

The cemetery grounds were somewhat neglected: graves overrun with weeds and weatherworn tombstones, to which I paid scant attention. If it were today, I would spend some time looking at the headstones, paying attention to the names and dates, but back then I just went straight to the Center without giving any thought to those souls in eternal sleep who were waiting in vain for the rare visit from a relative, friend, or even a passerby.

Maybe a cemetery in Romania, the country where Dracula and my paternal grandparents were born (I don't think they were acquainted), has found the solution for those poor souls waiting for a visit. Romania is home to the "Merry Cemetery." Each gravestone is carved in bright, cheerful colors and contains a poem, often with a humorous message from the person buried there. What better way to connect with someone, relative, friend, or unknown, who has gone over to "the other side?"

There were two advantages to going up Granada. It was shorter, and Aunt Mary and Uncle Bill lived on it, and I could stop to say hello (and be offered a piece of her delicious chocolate cake). Once when I stopped there, my cousin Sheldon was in the driveway washing his car, some kind of sports car.

Sheldon was eight years older than me. His nickname was "tank," probably because he was heavy-set, rather stout, and his last name was Sherman, which brought up the association with the famous World War Two "Sherman Tank." On that day, Aunt Mary called me in to have some cake. As I was sitting at the table, my fork raised about to convey a piece of cake into my mouth, Sheldon came in and said, "Let me introduce you to Fido."

Since I don't remember the real name, I've settled on Fido, a previously popular name for a dog, which also happened to be the name of Abraham Lincoln's dog. If Fido was good enough for Lincoln, then it's good enough for me. Now, Fido was a rather big German Shepherd who might've wanted to make my acquaintance, but the feeling wasn't mutual. When my cousin brought Fido in, he went under the table to examine my feet (Fido, not my cousin). Luckily, Sheldon pulled him away before he could "taste" them.

Uncle Bill had a parking lot downtown. Customers would leave their cars with the keys, and Uncle Bill would park them (the cars, not the customers). That gave him the ability to make the best use of the space, but it also meant being outside in the cold, snowy winter weather, which lasted from November to April.

I don't know if Uncle Bill liked, disliked, or only tolerated the cold weather in Youngstown, but my dad hated it, which is one of the reasons we moved to sunny California in 1964. Me? I liked the snowy weather: I didn't have to drive in it; I didn't have to shovel it (my dad did that); I was a kid, and kids like to play in the snow.

# CHAPTER 34

# JEWISH COMMUNITY CENTER (CONTINUED)

The Jewish Community Center (JCC) was a long, two-story building. Upstairs, there were meeting rooms. On the main floor there was a gymnasium with bleachers and basketball hoops for practice and competitions. There was a fitness room. Not even close to the fitness rooms of today. It consisted of a large mat and a set of barbells. I used to work out with a friend, really an acquaintance, by the name of Robbie Rosenbaum.

I was about fourteen, and Robbie was two or three years older. He was short but had been working out for a couple of years and was very muscular. You know those commercials advertising a bodybuilding program showing what someone looks like before and then after ten weeks of exercising using the program? They could've hired me and Robbie. I could've been the "before," and Robbie the "after."

Also downstairs, there was a large social gathering room with pool tables and ping-pong tables. On Saturday and Sunday afternoons, me and my friends would hang out there. But my favorite part of the JCC was the 25-yard heated indoor swimming pool, which was made possible by a donation in 1958 from the Schwebel family, owners of the Schwebel Bakery. (Boy, do they deserve a special thanks!) I loved that pool. I spent countless hours there. Every afternoon or evening during the summer.

There were two diving boards, the low and the high. I never had the nerve to go on the high dive, but my sister did, that is, until one evening when she was the last person in the pool, and the lifeguard, a young kid of about seventeen, thought it would be "great fun" to turn off all the lights while she was on the high board.

She didn't find it amusing. She was terrified. Imagine how it must've felt. You're at the edge of the high board, ten or fifteen feet above the water, about to dive, and then all of a sudden the lights go out. The room is now in total darkness, and you can't see a thing. Not even the diving board you're standing on. Somehow, she managed to slowly and cautiously crawl backwards to the ladder and climb down, but till today, some sixty years later, she finds that memory traumatic.

The JCC also had clubs for high school students. These clubs were called fraternities (for boys) and sororities (for girls), similar to what you find at American universities. There were three fraternities: CBA (Center Boys Association); AZA (from Hebrew letters); and Rodans (first three letters of temple Rodef Sholom and Anshe Emeth Synagogue).

I was in Rodans. I (incorrectly) remembered it as being called "Rodents." You know, those (mostly) small mammals like mice and squirrels. Looking back, I found it peculiar that our fraternity was named after animals typically considered pests, rather than choosing a name with positive connotations like "Tigers." Known for their strength and power, tigers were famously featured in the 1960s Esso gas company advertisements with the slogan "Put a tiger in your tank." It seemed like there was a gas station on every corner telling you to put a tiger in your tank.

But maybe Tigers wouldn't have been a good choice. Imagine someone from the Tigers fraternity meeting a girl and saying, "I'm in the Tigers fraternity, and you know, as Esso says, "Put a tiger in your tank." Not the best pick-up line. Here are some lines that me and my friends used (with limited success): "If you and I were socks, we'd make a great pair"; "Well, here I am! What are your other two wishes?"; and "Are you a time traveler? Because I can see you in my future."

Once you decided on a fraternity, you went through a pledging period before being officially accepted as a member, a period of time in which you were expected to "obey" the members who often asked you to do silly things. This was a way of showing how much you really wanted to become a member. There was never anything dangerous (as is sometimes the case at the college level).

I do have one pledging memory, but it wasn't with me. It was with a boy named Jack. It was a cold autumn day, and we were on a street corner, somewhere near Rayen High School. There wasn't any snow on the ground, but it was chilly, and everyone had a jacket on except Jack, who was in his shirtsleeves with a cigarette in his mouth. (Back then we thought smoking was a sign of being grown up; luckily, I never smoked.) I don't remember which fraternity he was pledging, but I do remember what he had been told to do: make out with the streetlight pole! We all had a good laugh. No embarrassments, just high school antics.

## CHAPTER 35

# JEWISH FOOD

**As I've said, I'm not a religious, practicing Jew.** I'm a secular Jew. Most secular Jews think of their Jewishness as a matter of culture. When they think of their Jewish culture, they think of the food, of the Yiddish or Hebrew language, and of some limited holiday observances. I love Jewish food. Here's a brief description of some of the foods that are part of my Jewish cultural heritage.

- **MATZAH.** Crispy unleavened bread eaten during Passover (the holiday that commemorates the liberation of the Israelites from Egyptian slavery).

- **MATZAH BALL SOUP.** A thin chicken broth with matzah balls (fluffy, dumpling-like balls made from matzah meal).

- **BORSCHT.** Red beet soup. It was always served cold with a large dollop of sour cream.

- **BAGELS.** A small, ring-shaped type of bread that's often topped with cream cheese and lox (smoked salmon).

- **GEFILTE FISH.** Fish balls made from minced fish mixed with eggs, breadcrumbs, and spices, simmered in fish stock.

- **PASTRAMI SANDWICH**. A sandwich of rye bread, mustard, coleslaw, and pastrami (a smoked beef that contains a lot of spices)

- **KUGEL**. A baked sweet casserole of egg noodles, cottage cheese, raisins, and apples.

- **LATKES**. Fried potato pancakes usually eaten with sour cream or applesauce.

- **BLINTZES**. Thin-rolled egg pancakes similar to crepes, filled with sweetened cheese, often topped with sour cream. Today I would top it with whipped cream. I have a weakness for whipped cream. Why is Thanksgiving my favorite holiday? Pumpkin pie smothered with whipped cream.

- **CHALLAH BREAD**. Braided bread (the dough is rolled into ropes, which are then braided) made with so many eggs that it is typically pale yellow in color and has a rich flavor.

- **CHICKEN SOUP** A traditional dish of the European Jewish kitchen. In American popular culture, chicken soup (sometimes dubbed "Jewish Penicillin") is thought of as the quintessential Jewish comfort food, a cure-all for colds, heartbreaks, or other physical or emotional ailments.

Brazilians also believe in the medicinal value of chicken soup, which they call "canja." They also have faith in another "surefire" remedy for coughs and colds: garlic tea with lemon in it, which I found to be a ghastly but surprisingly effective concoction.

Once, the year before I married Neusa, I came down with a bad cold. I had a runny nose, a cough, and was sneezing a lot. I was feeling miserable. Neusa came over to see me (I was living in an apartment behind the ICBEU) and brought me a thermos of this garlic tea. I took one whiff, effusively thanked her, and said I would take it after she left, at which time I confess (this memoir needs to be as truthful as possible) I poured it down the drain (and probably killed a cockroach or a spider or two).

One of my fondest memories is of dinners at my grandmother Dina Schulman's house on Selma Avenue. In the dining room, there was a long table at which all the adults sat. We kids (me, Maureen and Jeff, and our many cousins) sat at card tables in the living room just off of the dining room. The meal always began with appetizers. There was borscht and tomato juice. There was chopped liver (minced roasted chicken livers, mixed with hard-boiled eggs, onions, and spices), which we ate on crackers.

I don't remember eating liver as a main dish when I was growing up, but later in Brazil, Neusa and her mother often made it, frying it with onions. It may sound a little strange or exotic. But as far as strangeness goes, it's not alone. Here are some other foods you may (or may not) want to try: ant eggs (the Philippines); bats (Thailand); chicken feet (the Caribbean); cockroaches (Thailand); dog meat (Korea); monkey brains (China); tarantulas (Cambodia); and snails (France). Bon appetit!

There were also deviled eggs, hard-boiled eggs cut in half horizontally and filled with a paste made from the egg yolks mixed with mayonnaise and Dijon mustard and sprinkled with paprika. The word "deviled" doesn't refer to the Devil, but rather it refers to the spicy or zesty taste.

The main course was brisket (meat from the chest of a cow, cooked slowly in a small amount of liquid in a closed container) or chicken paprikash, a dish of Hungarian origin. My cousin Eric Chevlen remembers it as "a tomato and paprika-flavored thick gravy with chicken thighs in it." The main dish was always accompanied by kugel.

The meal was prepared by Bessy (Bessy Anglin, 1908–1983), a tall, medium-built African-American who, for many years, was the Aron/Schulman family cook, housekeeper, and caretaker, at least from as early as 1940 (at which time my mother was nineteen and my aunt Audrey was only seven) until 1965, the year of my grandmother's death.

I have fond memories of Bessy and would like to think she was considered part of the family (but I have no way of knowing if that was the case). We left Youngstown in 1964 when I was sixteen. In July of 1971, I traveled to Cleveland to attend my good friend Mark Newman's wedding. Before returning to Los Angeles, I went to Youngstown, and one evening at Aunt Helen's house, Bessy was there when I walked in. She was excited to see me, but I remember my response as being sedate and polite, without the enthusiasm I would show if somehow she were to appear before me today. Sadly, I didn't give her the attention she deserved.

# CHAPTER 36

# YIDDISH

**Although I went to Sunday School to learn** about Jewish history, culture, traditions, and the Hebrew language, I never learned much Hebrew. Sometimes the adults in the extended Aron family would say some things in Yiddish, a language used by Jewish people in central and eastern Europe. Here are a few common Yiddish words and expressions most American Jews will be familiar with.

- **CHUTZPAH**. Extreme arrogance, brazen audacity. Leo Rosten (1908–1997) in his book *The Joys of Yiddish* gives the perfect example of chutzpah: a man who kills his mother and father and asks the court for mercy because he's an orphan.

- **DRECK**. Trash, junk, crap. There's a lot of dreck on television these days. I miss the old family-friendly television shows, like the 1960s *Mister Ed, the Talking Horse.*

- **GELT**. Money. Maybe the title of Woody Allen's 1969 film should've been *Take the Gelt and Run.* (It was "*Take the Money and Run.*")

- **KIBITZ**. To make small talk or idle chatter; to give unwanted advice. The 1930 movie *The Kibitzer* was based on a play of the same name written by the Romanian-American actor, Emanuel Goldenberg (1893–1973), later known as Edward G. Robinson.

- **KINDER** Children. Our parents and grandparents sometimes referred to us kids as "the kinder."

- **MAZEL TOV**. Congratulations on a happy and significant occasion or event. Reportedly, when President Harry Truman's mother-in-law, known to be a difficult mother-in-law, died, Albert Einstein sent him a telegram with a single word on it: "Mazel Tov."

- **MENSCH**. A genuinely good, decent person; someone to admire and emulate. My Uncle Norman was a mensch.

- **MESHUGGENEH.** Crazy, ridiculous, insane. When Neusa and I got married, our plan was to travel from Panama to LA by bus. That was the most meshuggeneh idea I've ever had. But I think Neusa was even more meshuggeneh to agree to it.

- **OY VEY.** An expression of dismay or woe. *Oy Vey, Honey. I Shrunk the Kinder* (for a Yiddish version of the film).

- **SCHMUCK.** A fool, a stupid person. Literally, the word means "penis." Maybe the *Dumb and Dumber* film could've been called *Two Schmucks.*

CHAPTER 37

# EMPHASIS ON ACHIEVEMENT

**When I think of my Jewish heritage, the words** "success" and "achievement" come to mind. On the whole, Jews are successful.

Our parents stressed the importance of a college education, diploma, and career. There was never a doubt as to whether I would go to college. It was a given. It was also a given that I would have a professional career. Which reminds me of the story of the Jewish mother pushing a stroller with her two young boys in it. A passerby asks her how old they are, to which she replies, "The doctor is one, and the lawyer is two." Here are some Jews I think of when I think of success.

First of all, I think of my aunts and uncles. Uncles Harry, Norman, Jules, and Ed grew a small corner grocery store into a prominent regional supermarket chain, Century Foods; Uncle Bill had a parking lot; Uncle Marvin had a jewelry business; Uncle Morrie and Aunt Lil had a restaurant. Uncle Walter is a retired podiatrist. Uncle Harold was a doctor.

I think of my brother, who against all odds went to medical school (my parents didn't have any way to financially support him) and later went on to become Medical Director for Infection Control and Pharmacy at a major health care system in northern California. (He is nationally known within his field, and in 2023 was Sutter Health Physician Leader of the Year!) And to think all of this was possible thanks to my having once saved his life when he was a toddler. We were at a park in Los Angeles. Jeff was two and I was five. He began toddling towards the swings, and I ran and yanked him away just in time for him not to be hit by a ten-year-old kid who was "swinging away."

I think of my sister, who excelled in writing contemplative poetry, did theater work, taught young deaf adults, became a political activist, especially making sure people knew the importance of casting their votes, and danced professionally.

I think of my brother-in-law (Joel Shallit), my sister-in-law (Mindy Silvers), and my cousins. They all have had successful careers as doctors, lawyers, teachers, physical/occupational therapists, nurses, chefs, and businessmen (among other professions).

There was a small Jewish community in Manaus when I was there from 1972 to 2010; the members were all successful, and many made major contributions to the community. I can't help mentioning two of them.

Samuel Isaac Benchimol (1923–2002). In 1942, along with his brothers, he founded BEMOL, the most important chain of department stores in Manaus and, in fact, in the Amazon region. Samuel was an entrepreneur, an economist, a political scientist, a university professor, a researcher, and a writer (he wrote over thirty books and seventy articles). He was one of the leading experts on the Amazon (Amazonia; the Amazon region) and one of its fiercest and most respected defenders.

Moysés Benarrós Israel (1924–2016) was an example of Jewish success combined with benevolence, kindness, generosity, altruism, and public spirit. He was known for his light and gentle dealings with people, for his warmth and friendliness, and for his open and captivating smile. Here are just three of the many civic roles through which he contributed to the economic development and social well-being of the city, state, and region.

- Founder and director of the Federation of Industries of the State of Amazonas (FIEAM).

- Director of the philanthropic hospital Santa Casa de Misericórdia (charity hospital).

- Director of the Bank of the State of Amazonas (BEA).

I'll end with a short list of famous Jews: Actors (Adam Sandler, Harrison Ford); Actresses (Gal Gadot, Natalie Portman); Film Directors (Woody Allen, Steven Spielberg); Singers (Bob Dylan, Barbara Streisand); Composers (Felix Mendelson, George Gershwin, Gustav Mahler); Painters (Frida Kahlo, Mark Chagall); Authors (Franz Kafka, Philip Roth, Judy Blume); Scientists (Albert Einstein, Jonas Salk, Sigmund Freud); Supreme Court Justice Ruth Bader Ginsburg; and Fashion Designer Calvin Klein.

CHAPTER 38

# CADILLAC CHARLIE

Across the street from our house on Elm Street lived a boy named Steve. We were both the same age (around fourteen) and occasionally played together. The only reason I remember him is because of something he told me and an event that followed some months later.

We had two friends we occasionally played with, Chuckie (age twelve) and his brother Tommy (age ten). He asked me if I knew who their father was. I said I didn't. He then told me that their father was "Cadillac Charlie." I said, "So, their father is a used car salesman?" to which he replied, "No, he's in the Mafia. That's his Mafia nickname." As far as Maffia nicknames go, that was one of the duller ones. Here are a few more colorful Maffia nicknames.

- **TONY "JOE BATTERS" ACCARDO.** Due to his proficiency with a baseball bat when he was one of Al Capones's most dedicated "sluggers."

- **JOSEPH "HA HA" AIUPPA.** A notorious scowler not given to smiling.

- **LOUIS "PRETTY" AMBERG.** Called "Pretty" because he was so ugly that the Ringling Brothers Circus wanted to display him as the "missing link."

- **SAM "GOLF BAG" HUNT.** An Al Capone mob enforcer who concealed his automatic weapons in a golf bag when he was on murder missions.

- **ALVIN "CREEPY" KARPIS.** Given that nickname because of his sallow, dour-faced looks.

That was the last I heard or thought about Cadillac Charlie until a few months later. More precisely, the morning of Friday, November 23rd, 1962, the day after Thanksgiving (and exactly one year before President John Kennedy was assassinated).

There was no school that day, so Charlie was going to take his kids to football practice. Tommy was in the car, and Chuckie was approaching the car. Charlie put his key in the ignition, gave it a turn, and set off a bomb hidden under the car that blew the car and garage to bits. All that remained of the car and the brick garage was three feet of rubble. Charlie and Tommy died instantly. Chuckie survived but was hospitalized for three months and needed to have his hip replaced. I never saw Chuckie again after that.

But for those who had no idea of Charlie's real line of work, he was a family man, a good father, whose profession was "grape salesman" (which is how he presented himself when asked; better than saying "mob capo").

Cadillac Charlie's car-bomb death was only one of over eighty unsolved underworld bombings that gave rise to the phrase "Youngstown Tune-up" and to Youngstown getting its nickname, "Bomb Town." That was the only Maffia-related incident in my life, and my memories of Youngstown are all pleasant and nostalgic.

# PART FOUR:

# CALIFORNIA

# (1964-1967)

# CHAPTER 39

# CALIFORNIA HERE I COME

*California Here I Come* was a song made famous by Al Jolson. If you know who Al Jolson was, you're probably a "senior citizen," which is a polite term meaning someone who's sixty-five or older. Some less polite ways to say someone is old are "along in the years"; "getting on"; "over the hill"; "no spring chicken"; or the Brazilian expression, which is my favorite, "um pé na cova" (one foot in the grave).

Al Jolson (1886–1950) was born in Lithuania and came to the United States in 1894. He was a vaudeville performer (a type of entertainment popular from the 1880s to the 1950s in which there were many short performances of different kinds: singing, dancing, jokes, etc.). In 1927, he starred in *The Jazz Singer*, considered the first talking movie.

In 1964, my family moved to Los Angeles, more specifically to Van Nuys, a neighborhood in the San Fernando Valley. The San Fernando Valley, known simply as "The Valley," is an urbanized valley bounded by hills and mountains. It's known for its iconic film studios (Warner Bros. and Walt Disney Studios), and to my surprise, in the 1970s, it was also known for producing adult films, giving it the nickname "Porn Valley."

"Valley girl" (she's a Valley girl) originally was used to

describe a materialistic upper-middle-class adolescent girl from the San Fernando Valley, but later it expanded to mean any adolescent female who is superficial and spoiled, likes to frequent malls, and has a penchant for conspicuous consumption. This expression was coined by rock musician Frank Zappa (Mothers of Invention) in 1982 with the release of a single of that name, which featured his fourteen-year-old daughter, Moon Unit Zappa.

No, this isn't a joke. Frank Zappa really did name his daughter "Moon Unit." When I saw this, I thought, Why didn't Neusa and I come up with that name when we were deciding what to name Paula? Now that I think about it, I like the thought of "Moon Unit Paula."

Frank Zappa isn't the only celebrity to give their children unusual names. Here are a few others: Beyoncé *(Blue Ivy)*; Alicia Keys *(Egypt* and *Genesis)*; Sylvester Stallone *(Sage Moonblood)*; Alanis Morissette *(Onyx Solace, Ever Imre,* and *Winter Mercy)*; and Nicole Kidman *(Sunday)*.

In July of 1964 (age sixteen), I went to a National Boy Scout jamboree in Valley Forge, Pennsylvania. My dad had already flown out to California, and after the jamboree, I flew out to join him. My mother, brother, and sister joined us in September.

I had a nice two months alone with my father until the rest of the family came. We went to see the movie *Tom Jones,* which was playing at the famous Grauman's Chinese Theater on Hollywood Boulevard. I really enjoyed the movie, and decades later in Seattle, I convinced my kids to watch it on one of the cable stations. We didn't make it through fifteen minutes (they failed to see what I saw in the film), and now it's a family joke, me always suggesting *Tom Jones* when we're trying to decide on a movie to watch together. (For some reason I'm always outvoted.)

After a few weeks, my dad and I moved from the studio apartment he had rented into a bigger apartment on the corner of Fulton and Oxnard, awaiting the arrival of the rest of the family. It was a perfect location: one block to the left was our high school (Grant), and directly across the street was Los Angeles Valley College, a community college. The apartments were built around a swimming pool. You walked out your door, and volilà, there was the swimming pool, which was convenient, that is, unless you are a sleepwalker.

# CHAPTER 40

# CALIFORNIA FRIENDS

I met Stan Levinson on my first day of school at Grant High School. I was a senior, and he was a junior. After he graduated (1967), he went to UCLA, where we roomed together at Rieber Hall. In 1969, he moved to San Francisco and finished his studies at the University of California in Berkeley (UC Berkeley).

In December of 1970, Stan came back to Los Angeles to spend the holidays with his family. Unfortunately, his mother was quite ill at the time. After New Year's, Stan returned to San Francisco. In January (1971), I kept saying to myself, "I need to call Stan's mother and see how she's doing." And then I'd think, "I can't bring myself to do it. She's really sick." This inner debate, I want to call but am afraid to call, continued over a period of several weeks.

Finally, I made a decision to call. I was on campus. I walked back to my apartment, which was a twenty-minute walk, and called Stan's mother's house. To my surprise, Stan answered the phone. Me: "What are you doing back in LA?" Stan: "Why are you calling my mother's phone?" Me: "I wanted to see how she's doing." Stan: She died half an hour ago!"

I'm not sure how much I believe in the paranormal, but there are things that defy explanation. Stan's mother died almost at the exact moment when I finally resolved to make the call. I've often thought about that strange coincidence. Was there some kind of paranormal communication between my mind and Stan's mind? How can you explain that after several weeks of putting off making the call, I would finally resolve to call at the exact moment his mother was dying?

Bill Gray lived in the same apartment building as my family. We were the same age and soon became friends. In September of 1965, we both began Los Angeles Valley Community College, where he was vice-president of the Associated Student Union and a member of the Men's Honor Service Club, the Knights. Thanks to Bill, I also joined the Knights.

I met Elaine Harris (her maiden name) in 1966 when she was president of the Cornets, the Women's Honor Service Club equivalent to the Knights. We became good friends and were always studying together at the library.

One day, Bill came up to me and asked if there was "anything between me and Elaine." He knew we were always together, so he wanted to ask me before asking her out. I told him we were just friends and encouraged him to ask her out. They began dating and were married in September of 1968. Some years later, Bill and Elaine divorced (amicably), and Elaine remarried. And not only did Bill go to Elaine's wedding, but he also supplied the champaign. If it were me, I also would have toasted the bridal couple, offering them champagne laced with MiraLax.

Gerry Huybregts and Estella Rush were also friends from Valley College. Gerry was born in Australia and came to the United States at the age of twenty. However, I don't remember him having an Australian accent.

Two short stories about accents. The year was 1968. I struck up a conversation with a girl at a bus stop near campus (UCLA). I don't remember if I was just talking to talk or if I was "hitting on her." I said I thought she had such a charming accent, to which she replied that she had a speech defect. I sure "put my foot in my mouth!"

And then there's the time I was in the car with my brother. I was back from Brazil on a visit. All of a sudden, he pulled over, stopped the car, and began staring at me. I asked, "What's going on?" He replied, "You're speaking English with an accent." I thought, "Great! I haven't mastered Portuguese, and I'm unlearning English."

Back to Gerry and Estella. Gerry was president of the Valley College Associated Student Union, and Estella was his girlfriend. After Valley College, Gerry and Estella went to UCLA. Estella was a resident advisor in one of the dorms, and Gerry lived at home and would drive to school. One day he decided to "pop the question." He knew Estella would be borrowing his car later that day, so he wrote a note asking her to marry him and stuck it on the steering wheel. Gerry was lucky he didn't have to wait long for her answer and got an immediate "yes." A British man named Keith wasn't so lucky. He had to propose 8,500 times over twenty-four years before he finally got a "yes" from Beverly Redmond.

# CHAPTER 41

# GRANT HIGH SCHOOL

**In September of 1964, I began my senior year** at Grant High School, which was conveniently located about two blocks from the apartment we were living in.

Grant is named after Ulysses S. Grant, president of the United States from 1869–1877. In 1865, as Commanding General in the American Civil War, he led the Union Army to victory against the Confederate Army. However, Grant almost didn't live to become president. President Lincoln invited Grant to join him to watch the play *Our American Cousin* at Ford's Theater. Grant made a polite excuse for not joining him, but the real reason was his wife detested Lincoln's wife. That animosity almost certainly saved Grant's life. John Wilkes Booth, who assassinated Lincoln that evening, April 14, 1865, had also planned to kill Grant at the same time.

Grant was a big school. There were over three thousand students, compared to the 1,200 students at Rayen. My graduating class alone had 840 students. At that time, many (or maybe the majority) of the students were Jewish.

Grant had a unique system for the students to enroll in the classes they wanted to take. On enrollment day, you had to literally run to each classroom and get your name on the enrollment sheet for the class. It was chaos because everyone was running to get to their desired classrooms. You would sign up for a class and then run to try to get a place in the next class on your list.

My Spanish teacher, Mr. Pilafas, was a young man, about twenty-two years old, of Greek descent. I really enjoyed his classes. However, there was one slightly unpleasant incident. In Spanish, there are two forms of "you": "usted" (used in formal situations and as a form of respect) and "tu" (which is informal and used between friends of the same age and social status). I wasn't aware of this distinction, and one day I addressed him as "tu." He almost bit my head off, telling me to never address him in this disrespectful manner. He could've corrected me in a different way, but nevertheless, I have pleasant memories of him as a teacher and of his classes.

Another class I really enjoyed was world literature. Stan and I had this class together. Our teacher was Mr. Cousins, and as Stan once commented, only an inspiring teacher like Mr. Cousins could make the old Greek plays with Oedipus, Agamemnon, and Antigone interesting.

I also had two practical subjects: typing and driver's education. The driver's ed class had two components. For some classes we would sit at simulators, something like an arcade video game with a steering wheel and a screen. The second component was actually driving. I think my driver's ed teacher must've been very religious because every time I was behind the wheel he seemed to lift up his eyes to heaven and pray.

I graduated on June 18, 1965, with a major in foreign languages (Spanish)—college preparatory, meaning the courses I took were meant to prepare me to continue my education in a community college or a university. I just discovered my diploma says I graduated "with honors." Also, to my surprise, I was number 141 in the class of 840. Not great, but pretty good.

All of the high schools that held their graduation ceremony that evening jointly rented Disneyland for the night. So, after the graduation ceremony we boarded charter buses for an all-night celebration at Disneyland. It was a good way to finish my high school years.

Famous people who studied at Grant include musicians Micky Dolenz (The Monkees) and Barry Melton of Country Joe and the Fish, an American psychedelic rock band. One of the songs they sang at Woodstock in 1969 was *I Feel Like I'm Fixin' to Die*, a dark, humorous, satirical protest against the war in Vietnam. Here are some of the lyrics:

> Well, come on all of you, big strong men,
> Uncle Sam needs your help again.
> He's got himself in a terrible jam
> Way down yonder in Vietnam
>
> So put down your books and pick up a gun,
> We're gonna have a whole lotta fun.
>
> And it's one, two, three,
> What are we fighting for?
> Don't ask me, I don't give a damn,
> Next stop is Vietnam;
>
> And it's five, six, seven,
> Open up the pearly gates,
> Well there ain't no time to wonder why,
> Whoopee! we're all gonna die.

CHAPTER 42

# VALLEY COLLEGE

In September of 1965, I entered Los Angeles Valley College, a community college conveniently located across the street from the apartment my family was living in.

A number of well-known (future) actors studied there, although none of them were my classmates. One of them was Sean Astin (Samwise Gamgee in *The Lord of the Rings* films). I never read the books or watched the films. I don't like books with strange, almost unpronounceable names, such as Frodo Baggins and Meriadoc Brandybuck. But come to think of it, I could've used those names with my kids: Sérgio Frodo, David Meriadoc, and Paula Galadriel.

I was a member of the Knights (the Men's Honor Service Club) and was president of the Spanish club, elected by a landslide. (OK. There were only ten students in the club, but since it was unanimous, I can still claim it was a landslide win.)

I did well at Valley College. I graduated cum laude (with honors) in June of 1967. For my good grades, my participation in the Knights, and my work as president of the Spanish club, I was awarded a certificate of leadership (spring of 1967) and a service scholarship of $150, which today would be the equivalent of $1,300.

My physical geography class teacher would show us slides of mountains, rivers, glaciers, fjords, etc. After viewing the fifth mountain, almost everyone in the class was half-asleep (a dark room and the picture of a mountain no different than the last four will do that to you). But our teacher had an infallible solution to capture the class's attention: he would quickly flash a slide with a picture from *Playboy*. Everyone (at least the boys) immediately sprang to attention, only to discover that the teacher had already moved on to the next slide of whatever geographic formation we were studying.

My World Lit teacher looked a little like the great Russian-American *The King and I* actor Yul Brynner (1920–1985). Now, at age seventy-six, when I look in the mirror, I see Woody Allen looking back at me. Why couldn't I just look like Tom Cruise?

What I most remember from his class is a comment he made during our discussion of Saint Augustine's *Confessions*. He said something to the effect of, "In life we make mistakes, but we can always make amends and go on to become a better person." His remark was meant as a prescription for conducting our lives: we should take responsibility for our wrong actions and make an attempt to rectify them.

The truth is everyone, at one time or another, does something (or fails to do something) that they regret. Perhaps it was a less-than-kind remark, perhaps a failure to give needed support, perhaps not thanking someone for something. A quote from St. Augustine: "There is no saint without a past, no sinner without a future." That's why in the Catholic religion there's confession, and in the Jewish religion we have Yom Kippur, known as the Day of Atonement.

I'm pretty good (but not perfect) at acknowledging when

I've done something I wish I hadn't and apologizing for it. I even apologized to a friend for something I had said more than thirty years earlier.

In October of 1970, Alan Witchner, one of my closest friends in Youngstown, suddenly passed away at the age of twenty-four. Alan's sister, Annie, was devastated and came to California to spend a short time with relatives.

My dad took me to pick her up so that we could spend some time together. When we ran to hug each other, she was crying. It was then that I said one of the stupidest things I've ever said. Actually, it was the stupidest thing I've ever said. I've said some doozies, but this "takes the cake." I said, "You can't cry forever." Maybe I should've had a tattoo on my forehead saying, "Danger: Mouth operates faster than brain." Some thirty-five years later, I found Anne on Facebook and sent an apology.

In a similar vein, I believe it's important to forgive those who, in our view, have wronged us. (Of course there are some things that would be hard to forgive, but for most things forgiveness is possible and desirable.) In the words of St. Augustine: "If you are suffering from a bad man's injustice, forgive him lest here be two bad men."

I'm good at forgiving. I can honestly say I don't feel animosity or resentment towards anyone. I have no grudges. Any and all who have passed through my life would be warmly received if today they were to show up at my door.

Enough of my more serious thoughts. Let me end with another quote from St Augustine: "Oh Lord, give me chastity, but do not give it yet."

# CHAPTER 43

# BAG BOY

**The year was 1965. My dad worked in the** furniture department at Fedco (Federal Employees Distributing Company), a membership department store that operated in Southern California from 1948 to 1999. Fedco was a one-stop shopping destination where the customer/member was presented with a wide variety of products: clothing, footwear, housewares, jewelry, furniture, appliances, sporting goods, hardware, toys, and groceries. It was the precursor (such an important-sounding word) of stores like Sam's Club and Target.

Fedco had a big grocery department, and it was there that I had what was really my first job. Dad talked to the grocery department manager, and I was hired as a bag boy. My job was to put the customers' groceries in bags and get the bagged groceries to their cars. It was a great part-time job for a seventeen-year-old kid. It paid well: $1.65 an hour. Today (2024), a supermarket bagger in Seattle earns about $15 an hour, but back then $1.65 was a good wage.

It was hard work. The cashiers were fast. I mean, really fast. They didn't even look at the cash register. One hand took the items and tossed them towards the bagger, and the other hand rang up the order, the fingers automatically punching the correct keys. Today everything is scanned. But in the time it takes a cashier to scan an item today, a cashier back then could ring up two or three items! So we bag boys had to be fast.

And fast we were. There were no plastic bags. Only paper bags, which we would open quickly in a way that always produced a very loud pop. Sadly, today an innocent and playful sound like that would have everyone in panic, the store in lockdown, the building surrounded by a SWAT team.

My hours were from five to nine several days a week. It was a twenty-minute walk to the bus stop and then a twenty-minute bus ride to the store. I didn't mind the bus ride. I used the time to read. Did I read ancient Greek or Roman classics, such as *The Odyssey* or *The Aeneid*? No. Did I read the great Spanish and Russian novels *Don Quixote* or *Crime and Punishment?* No. Did I read classics of American literature, such as *The Scarlet Letter* or *Moby-Dick?* No.

So what did I read? I would read a Spanish dictionary. My high school Spanish teacher had asked us to buy a monolingual Spanish dictionary, and I really did enjoy browsing through it. At least I wasn't reading a book that had been banned. But maybe I should've chosen a banned book. Here are some classics that at one time or another have been banned: *The Adventures of Huckleberry Finn; The Great Gatsby; Gone with the Wind; Lolita; The Absolute True Diary of a Part-Time Indian;* and *Tarzan.*

Maybe I should read *Tarzan* to see why it was banned. I always thought there was more to the famous but never-actually-spoken movie line "Me Tarzan, You Jane." I wonder what Jane did to Tarzan that caused him to emit that iconic Tarzan yell, which sounded like a wounded animal crying out in pain. Or maybe like the mating call of a forlorn ape.

I have two memories of my first day on the job, a first day that was almost my last. As I was bagging groceries for one of the cashiers, one of the other bag boys came up to me and said, "I'll pack these groceries. Find the manager and tell him we need a sky hook." When I found the manager and relayed the request, he burst out laughing: There's no such thing as a sky hook. The older bag boy was just having a little fun with "the new kid on the block."

This reminds me of the time a few years earlier (1962) when I was the one playing the joke on a younger, unsuspecting friend, my cousin Eric Chevlen. I told him I was going to induct him into a secret society, the Royal Siam Society. I then had him repeat (with dignified bows) the solemn incantation that would admit him into the society: OWA TAGOO SIAM! (I was such a nice cousin!)

Towards the end of my shift that day, I made a mistake that almost cost me my job. I was working out back behind the store loading groceries into the customers' cars. At the checkout, the bagger would put the groceries in paper bags and put the bags in tubs—three bags to a tub. The customers would get a card with a number corresponding to the number on the tub. A conveyor belt would take the tubs out to the area behind the store where the customers would drive up and present their card or cards. Those of us working out back would then match the cards to the tubs and put the groceries in the customers' cars. Can you see where this is going? In my haste to get the job done as fast as possible, I confused 21 with 12, meaning that the person who gave me card #21 got #12's groceries. Well, luckily I was given a second chance, and boy was I careful after that!

# CHAPTER 44

# BOY SCOUTS: MEXICO CITY

In the summer of 1965 (age 17), I went to Mexico City to help in the preconference preparations for the XX World Scout Conference (September 27–October 3). The World Scout Conference is the general assembly of the World Organization of National Scout Organizations. I went to Mexico City on July 12th and returned in the first week of September. I would have liked to have stayed for the conference, but I was starting college (Los Angeles Valley College) in September.

I had studied Spanish in high school, was about to graduate, and planned to go to college and become a Spanish teacher. I thought it would be a good idea to go to Mexico for the summer and live with a family who had a Scout my age. It would be a great opportunity for me to meet Scouts from Mexico and improve my rudimentary knowledge of Spanish.

I wrote a letter to the American National Scout Office asking if there was any way I could go to Mexico and spend the summer with a Scout family. The National Scout office forwarded my request to the Mexican National Scout Office in Mexico City, which responded they would be happy to receive me, that I could stay with a Scout family, and that I would help with the preconference work. That was the first time I learned about the conference.

My host family was a Jewish family in the Lomas de Chapultepec neighborhood, an exclusive neighborhood known for its mansions and wealthy residents. I confess, I should've been a better houseguest. I acted almost as if I was living in a hotel, just a place to sleep. One of my regrets. Contrary to popular belief, I'm not a saint. I had (and, alas, still have) my faults (but I do try to be the kind of decent and considerate person we would like our daughters to marry). So, if you want to read about a saint, buy *A Treasury of Saints: 100 Saints, Their Lives and Times* by Malcolm Day.

Other than helping sort mail by region and country, I don't remember what my duties were. I spent a lot of time talking with everyone in the office in Spanish, and by the time I left, my Spanish had improved quite a bit. This was probably helped by the fact that there were a number of "muchachas" of around eighteen or nineteen years of age working as secretaries (this proves that motivation is key to learning a second language, if you know what I mean).

One day, about two weeks before I returned to Los Angeles, I was standing next to the desk of Roberto Reyes, one of the Scout executives, when all of a sudden the room seemed to tilt. Some of the secretaries began to cry. Roberto said (in Spanish), "It's a small earthquake. Remain calm." It didn't last long, and soon we were all back doing whatever we had been doing before the quake.

I don't remember it as having been particularly scary. But six years later, I would have an entirely different experience, an experience that was absolutely terrifying. It happened on Tuesday, February 9, 1971, at 6 a.m. I was blissfully asleep in my apartment near UCLA, perhaps lost in a serene dream, picturing myself "in a boat on a river with tangerine trees and marmalade skies," inspired by the Beatles song *Lucy in the Sky with Diamonds.* Or maybe it was a dream about one of my angelic, saintly girlfriends. Or one of my not-so-saintly girlfriends.

I was rudely awakened from my slumber. First there was a sharp jolt. Then the shaking began, first slowly, then faster and faster and faster, the shaking growing increasingly more and more violent. Everything was rattling—the windows, the doors, the pots and pans in the kitchen, my brain. The noise was thunderous! It sounded and felt like a train was coming through the apartment.

Then it stopped. It had lasted about twelve seconds. Twelve very lonnnnng seconds. We went outside. Everyone in all of the apartments out on the street in their pajamas. This quake measured 6.6 on the Richter Scale. Sixty-five people lost their lives, more than two thousand were injured, and eighty thousand homes or businesses were damaged or destroyed.

Sometime around the first week in September, I returned to Los Angeles. I sold my plane ticket and bought a bus ticket. I wanted to use the money to buy a camera. My mother was in Youngstown visiting her family. There was a friend of the family who had a camera store. I sent my mother the money I got from exchanging my air ticket, and she bought me a 35-millimeter camera (of course digital cameras weren't even a dream at that time). I have no idea how I sent her the money. Back then, internet bank transfers didn't exist. Maybe I sent a money order via Western Union. Or maybe by telekinesis, the ability to move an object with your mind.

Speaking of telekinesis, that reminds me of an unusual

antiwar protest against the Vietnam War in June of 1967, led by activists/counterculture icons Jerry Rubin (1938–1994) and Abbie Hoffman (1936–1989). Several hundred protesters encircled the Pentagon, chanting ancient Aramaic exorcism rites, intending to get the building to "rise into the air, turn orange, and vibrate until all evil emissions had fled." Here's a condensed part of the incantation they chanted that day:

> "We call upon the powers of the cosmos to protect our ceremonies in the name of Zeus; in the name of the lives of the soldiers in Vietnam who were killed because of a bad karma; in the name of Dionysus, Jesus, Yahweh; in the name of the flowing living universe, we call upon the spirit to raise the Pentagon…"

Well, the Pentagon refused to cooperate. Maybe there was a mistake in the incantation (or in something they had smoked).

# CHAPTER 45

# BACK TO MEXICO CITY

**In June of 1966, I returned to the Boy Scout** office in Mexico City. I arrived on June 20th. I stayed with another Jewish family, the Perez Solis family. Their son Efrain was a Scout about my age who worked in the Mexican National Scout office. His parents, Salvador and Sofia, were the Mexican version of a semi-autobiographical book that was made into a film in 1950. And what book and film might that be? *Cheaper by the Dozen.* The book describes the daily lives and childhood adventures of the authors, who grew up in the early 20th century in a household with twelve children.

Here's the incident in the book that gave rise to the title. The father of the family and his twelve children were out driving. He stopped at a red light, and a pedestrian asked, "Hey, mister! How come you got so many kids?" He pretended to ponder the question, and then just as the light turned green, he said, "Well, they come cheaper by the dozen, you know," and drove off.

Can you see where I'm going? Salvador and Sofia had twelve children! (which beats my grandmother, who had nine). And still they had room for me to stay with them. They weren't a rich family. They lived in a small, three-bedroom apartment. All of the children had biblical names. Here are a few: Efrain, Esther, Isaac, Abraham, and Yahel.

I stayed with them until the 2nd of July, at which time I took a bus to San Antonio, Texas. San Antonio is named for the Portuguese priest Saint Anthony of Padua. In Brazil, Saint Anthony (Santo Antônio) is known as a "matchmaking" saint. June 12th, the eve of Saint Anthony's Day, is Brazilian Valentine's Day, "Dia dos Namorados," which translates as "Sweetheart's Day." (It was on this day in 1973 that I asked Neusa's father for his blessing for me to marry Neusa.)

From San Antonio, I took a Greyhound bus to Youngstown, Ohio, to visit family and friends. I stayed with Aunt Helen and Uncle Harold. I wanted to take a shower right away (after those days on the bus, I was a little "smelly"; "stinky" would be more accurate), but they insisted that I eat something first.

I spent the month of July and most of August in Youngstown and then took a bus back to Los Angeles (two days and nine hours on the bus). The truth is, I should have spent the summer in Los Angeles working at my job as a bag boy at Fedco, where I worked after school.

# CHAPTER 46

# HIGH SIERRAS

**The summer of 1966 was also my last** Scout camping adventure. Every year (beginning in 1941), Los Angeles radio station KFI sponsors a camping trip for Eagle Scouts in the wilderness of California's Sierra Nevada mountains (the High Sierras). That year I was one of twenty Eagle Scouts awarded the trip.

We left the KFI Studio in Burbank on Friday evening, September 2nd, in a chartered bus and arrived at our starting point, Horse Corral, in Sequoia National Park, at 3 a.m. We piled out of the bus and sacked out on the ground in our sleeping bags, with the stars above for our tent. Then somehow we managed to "rise and shine" at 8 a.m. (Between our excitement and the invigorating mountain air, we were soon wide awake.) We were introduced to the burros that had been rented for the trip (pleased to meet you) and given a demonstration on how to pack them. (The burros carried all of our food and the cooking gear.) Cooking was done by camp trail chef John Robinson. Some typical meals he prepared:

- Orange juice, prunes, bacon, flapjacks, and cocoa.

- Ground beef patties, Spanish rice, peas, and butterscotch pudding.

- Split pea soup, baked ham, cabbage, corn bread with

butter and honey, and Sierra salad.

Although we only hiked three or four miles a day, it was over some very rough and challenging terrain. There was a part of the trail that was quite narrow, with a high rock wall on one side and sheer drops on the other. Very scary. For me, the high point of the trip, both literally and figuratively, was Elizabeth Pass (elevation 11,200 feet). That's higher than Pico da Neblina (9,827 feet), the highest mountain in Brazil. We returned to the KFI studio on September 10th, bone-tired but exhilarated after nine days and fifty-five miles of hiking in the beautiful High Sierra wilderness.

That really was the end of my time in the Boy Scouts. My interest faded and turned to activities at Los Angeles Valley College.

# PART FIVE:

# CALIFORNIA

# (1967-1971)

# CHAPTER 47

# UCLA

**In September of 1967, I entered UCLA** (the University of California at Los Angeles) as a junior, majoring in Spanish language and literature. Two years later, in June of 1969, I graduated with a Bachelor of Arts degree. In September of 1969, I began working on a master's in Spanish and, at the same time, a State of California Standard Teaching Credential so that I could teach Spanish and ESL (English as a Second Language) in middle schools and high schools. I received my teaching credential in June of 1970 and my master's four years later in June of 1974.

UCLA is one of ten campuses of the University of California system. It began in 1919 in Hollywood as the Southern Branch of the University of California. In 1927, the university broke ground for its new campus in Westwood and officially took the name UCLA. But some wits have given other meanings: Under Construction Like Always; United Colon Lovers Association; and Ugly Cheerleaders, Lousy Athletes.

In the spring quarter of 1968, I took a 2-credit dance class on the national dance of Chile, "La Cueca." This dance is a parody of the courtship of a chicken and a rooster. The dancers wave handkerchiefs above their heads, symbolizing the feathers of the chicken or the rooster's comb. I don't think I was a particularly good rooster, but I did pass the course.

Spring quarter of 1969 was my last quarter before graduating in June. I had completed all of my required credits, so I was able to take two electives. I chose elementary Portuguese and elementary Japanese. I have no memories of my Japanese class. But there's a little story about my attempt to speak Japanese. (If you want to speak another language, you should look for opportunities to speak it and not be afraid of making mistakes.)

There's a neighborhood in downtown Los Angeles called Little Tokyo. It's a Japanese commercial district consisting of shops and restaurants. Great, I thought. I'll go there and practice my Japanese. So, I went and entered a little shop. I gave a traditional bow and said, *"Kon'nichiwa."* (good afternoon). The little middle-aged Japanese shopkeeper gave me a surprised look and answered, *"Kon'nichiwa."* I was encouraged. I continued, *"O genki desu ka?"* (How are you?) Still with a surprised look, she answered, *"Genki desu"* (I am fine). I thought, "Oh wow! I'm really communicating in Japanese." So I decided to say the most complex sentence I knew in Japanese. I bowed, pointed to myself, and said, *"Kore wa watashi no shats desu"* (this is my shirt), to which she replied in perfect unaccented English: "So what?"

In June of 1971, I began work on my master's thesis, which had the exciting title of *Derived Modifiers in Spanish: A Semantic Analysis.* If you think that's a weird topic, look at a paper published in the *Journal of Analytical Psychology:* "Farting as a Defense against Unspeakable Dread." I dread flying, so maybe it wouldn't be advisable to sit next to me on a plane.

For my thesis, every adjective in a well-known Spanish and English dictionary was put on an index card (giving me about two thousand cards). These adjectives were then organized into sets according to their suffixes. Then the adjectives within each suffix set were classified into semantic subsets, that is, into subsets based on their meanings. Phew!! Maybe I should've been a psychology major and investigated farting.

My thesis supervisor was Dr. William E. Bull. Dr. Bull was very generous with his time; his office door was always open. Once in his office, you were greeted by two objects that were invariably on his desk: an ashtray overflowing with cigarette butts (he smoked like a chimney) and his cowboy hat (he was an academic with a cowboy persona).

Another teacher was Dr. Bárcia. Of him and his classes, I have just one memory: in relation to something we had just read, he said (in Spanish): "When we look back on our lives, everything in the past seems to have happened in the blink of an eye." Back then it didn't really register with me, but now at the age of seventy-seven, I say How true! How true!

I also remember he had a cute daughter who also studied at UCLA, but that speaks more to his genes than to his teaching (but he was an excellent teacher).

Both Dr. Bull and Dr. Barcia wrote books for learners of Spanish, and both books were being used at UCLA at the same time. So we students needed an easy way to differentiate the Bull books from the Bárcia books. Our solution: one course was labeled "Bullshit" and the other "Bárcia-shit"!

# CHAPTER 48

# ROOMMATES

**Between 1967 and 1971, I had a number of** roommates. With one or two exceptions, it was an experience that varied between good and great.

My first roommate was Stan Levinson, my first and best California friend. We roomed together at UCLA in Rieber Hall from the fall of 1967 to the end of the spring quarter of 1968. Rieber was a seven-story structure. There were two wings, one for men and the other for women. On the ground floor there was a cafeteria/dining hall, the front desk, a TV room, several small study rooms, and a large lounge with several comfortable sofas for relaxing (and if you were lucky, for making out).

Our room was on the third floor. There were around four hundred men and four hundred women living in Rieber Hall. Each floor had thirty rooms, two students to a room, and two large bathrooms with communal showers. There were four dorms in this part of the campus, so that means there were about three thousand students. Three thousand hormone-flooded college students!

I was beginning my junior year, having done my first two years at Los Angeles Valley Community College. Stan was in his sophomore year, initially majoring in French, which he later changed to Latin American Studies. He brought his stereo and his LP vinyl record collection. It was through Stan that I first heard Cream, the Bee Gees, and the Four Tops.

I decorated the wall on my side of the room with centerfolds from *Playboy*. Do I hear gasps of surprise? I was a normal male college student. In 1967, *Playboy* wasn't obscene or racy. It was actually quite "tame," and it decorated the walls of many male college dorm rooms, so I was far from the exception.

The next year (fall of 1968 to spring quarter of 1969) was my senior year. Stan had decided to live at home, so I had a different roommate. We never became friends. I don't even remember his name. But there's one incident that comes to mind. It was around midnight. We were both asleep. The phone rang. He answered it and handed it to me, saying it was for me. It was my brother calling to say that our father had just had a heart attack and was in the hospital. I told him what had happened, and he just said, "OK," and went back to sleep. It was as if my brother had called to say he heard it was going to rain tomorrow. My brother picked me up, and we went to the hospital. My dad survived the heart attack and some years later had a bypass operation. He died from cancer in 1980, at the age of sixty-six.

In the fall of 1969 until the spring quarter of 1970 (age twenty-one), I lived in Mira Hershey Hall, a residence hall for graduate students. My roommate was Dean Mollner. He was a first-year med student. He was also a little crazy, in a nice way. He was the one who decorated our room. (No more *Playboy* centerfolds. I was now a "mature"?? grad student.)

Here's how our room looked. On his side of the room, he hung a huge psychedelic painting he had made using fluorescent paints. Above the painting and shining on it was a long black light. At night, when the lights were off, turning on this black light would make the painting glow brightly.

He removed the light fixture from the ceiling and replaced it with a biforked unit that looked like an inverted Y. One part of the Y had a red bulb and the other a blue bulb. So, when the lights were turned on, you would see a red and a blue light. But he didn't stop there. He installed a flashing device so that the lights would alternately flash red or blue! You can imagine how our room looked at night from the street: the huge glowing psychedelic painting and the blinking red and blue lights. It was always Christmas in our room! (And for the record, neither of us ever smoked pot.)

From September of 1970 until December of 1971 (one month before I went to Brazil), I lived in an apartment off campus, about one block from the International Student Center (ISC) and about twenty minutes from the heart of the campus. The apartment was on the second floor. The front room served as the living room and my bedroom. The couch was my bed.

In order to be able to pay for a place, I had to have roommates. I knew what kind of roommates I wanted: international students studying at UCLA. My first roommates were Liberato Salandanan and Kwami Assuming. Liberato was from the Philippines, and Kwami was from Ghana.

A number of others came in as roommates. Dang Tran moved in the summer of 1971. Dang is from Vietnam. He is without a doubt the most practical, level-headed, down-to-earth person I know, and we are still in touch after all these years.

There was a guy from China. He would always get up at 4 a.m. to study. His desk was in the living room (which you'll remember is where I slept), so after a while, I would also get up at that time and study. There was a guy from Turkey, but this isn't a pleasant memory because we had a major argument (I don't remember what it was about), and he didn't stay long. In retrospect, I wish things had been different.

Finally, I even had a suitcase for a roommate. A guy from Czechoslovakia wanted to pay rent for his suitcase. I said, "What do you mean?" He replied that he was living with his girlfriend and might need a place if his girlfriend kicked him out.

CHAPTER 49

# STAN TELLS ME NOT TO BE A SCHMUCK

**Schmuck is a Yiddish word. Literally, it means** "penis." Of course, Stan wasn't telling me to stop acting like a penis (but maybe he was). He was telling me to stop acting like a jerk, which is the common meaning of schmuck. This word isn't vulgar; most people (unless you're Jewish) don't even know the literal meaning.

It was sometime in early 1968 when we were roommates at UCLA. My parents were going through a divorce. At that time, my dad worked as a parking enforcer at UCLA. He would drive around the university, giving tickets to people who parked illegally or whose parking time had expired. My dad was in a lot of emotional pain. He would come to my dorm's dining hall and have dinner with me. He would talk about the pending divorce and how sad he was. Listening to him and his suffering affected me, and my stomach would be in knots.

Then, one day I walked into the dining hall, saw my dad sitting alone at a table, and walked over to another table to sit with Stan and some of his friends. When I got to Stan's table, he looked at me and said, "Don't be a schmuck. Go sit with your father." Without a word, I turned around and went to sit with my dad.

I wound up "taking sides" with my dad and couldn't even bear to talk with my mother. I essentially stopped talking to her. Then I got a letter from my mother's sister, my Aunt Helen. That letter changed everything. She said that I should try to be more understanding, that this wasn't easy for my mother either, that she was also suffering but felt that she couldn't continue in the marriage. My aunt told me how much my mother loved me and how hurt she was because I had stopped all communication. Nudged by my aunt's letter, I called my mother and reestablished communication. Saved by Aunt Helen.

I didn't realize how much my father was suffering, how much he was hurting. This realization came home in a sad way in February of 1969. I got a call from my mother saying my father was in the hospital. He had overdosed on sleeping pills. Uncle Norman immediately flew down to Los Angeles to give us (me, my brother, and sister) emotional support.

My father survived. A psychologist at the hospital told us that our father would recover emotionally, but it would take time. My dad did recover emotionally. He remade his life and rented a one-bedroom apartment, not far from Los Angeles Valley College.

During that time, a new person, Bill Van Holt, came into my mother's life. When I was introduced to him, he extended his hand for us to shake hands. And me? I withdrew my hand and put it behind my back! Although I was now on good terms with my mother, I wasn't prepared for a stepfather. But eventually I did accept Bill.

Bill and Mom rented an apartment not far from where my father was living. I helped with the moving in. Their apartment was on the second level, up a flight of stairs. My brother, who was still living at home, had an upright piano, which was, as you can imagine, quite heavy. I helped (pushing from behind) get the piano up the stairs. That day, when we struggled together to get that heavy piano up the stairs, was the day I finally accepted Bill.

So here we are at some point in late 1969. My father is doing well and, for all practical purposes, has recovered from the divorce. He would later find someone, Millie, to share his life. Mom and Bill would eventually divorce, and Mom would marry for a third time (Darrel Hiles). So this story does have a happy ending. In fact, you could even say I reaped an unexpected benefit from my parents' divorce. Occasionally I would come home for a weekend. I would first have dinner at my dad's and then walk the several blocks to my mother's and have a second dinner.

# CHAPTER 50

# MORE CALIFORNIA FRIENDS

**Sharon Grant was a friend from Valley College.** After Valley College, we both went to UCLA, where she was an engineering major. We both lived in Rieber Hall (1968). Early one evening, she called me. She had a problem and wanted my advice. She had accepted two dates for the same evening and didn't know what to do. I don't remember what I suggested. I could've told her I had a different problem: I had two evenings and no dates.

This may surprise you, but I was friends with Tom Brady. Okay. It wasn't Brazilian supermodel Gisele Bundchen's Tom Brady, the famous NFL player. This was at Los Angeles Valley College in 1965, twelve years before the "famous" Tom Brady was even born. Nevertheless, I can claim I was a friend of Tom Brady, and I wouldn't be lying.

My friend Tom Brady was more the size of a football than a football player: he was short and stocky. Tom was a good friend, but his girlfriend, Carol, didn't seem to like me. I couldn't imagine why. Then I discovered why. Here's how it happened.

The year was early 1970. I was living in Hershy Hall, the dorm for graduate students. I got a call. Tom and Carol were in the lobby. I went down and greeted Tom, saying, "Hey, long time no see!" to which Carol said, "But you were with him last weekend," at which point Tom, unperceived by Carol, gave me a slight kick to my shoe. Which prompted me to reply, "Yes. I've been studying so much I completely forgot." So, I finally found out why Tom's girlfriend didn't like me: every time Tom wanted to go out with someone else, he would tell her he wasn't going to see her because he was doing something with me. I was his excuse, or should I say, his "cover-up"?

Steve Schimmel. It was fall of 1971. I was a graduate student working on my master's in Spanish. I had an apartment, which I shared with several roommates. My apartment was on the second floor, and Steve lived alone in an apartment directly below mine.

One evening I was at my desk trying to study. The floor began to vibrate, and my apartment was inundated with the sounds of classical music. Steve had just bought a new stereo and was playing it at top volume. I had never met him. I went down and asked if he could please turn down the volume. That's how our friendship began. I considered Steve a good friend, but unfortunately our friendship ended due to something I did. A real blunder.

Steve was having problems with his girlfriend and would always call me to come down to give him advice. I don't know what gave him the idea that I (at twenty-three) was savvier about "affairs of the heart" than he was (at twenty-eight). I had had a few girlfriends, but nothing serious, and at the time I was "unattached," which is better than being "unhinged."

Steve was very religious. His girlfriend was also religious, and they would often pray together. In the summer, Los Angeles is quite hot. Our building and the adjacent buildings didn't have air conditioning. Our air conditioning was open windows and a hope for a breeze. So, one day Steve and his girlfriend were praying fervently. Since it was summer and windows were open, everyone could hear their prayers. When they finished praying, some girls in the building next door clapped (fervently) and shouted, "Keep up the good work!"

So what was my blunder that ended our friendship? It was around 1979. I was living in Brazil. A friend was going to the States. I recorded an audio tape for my friends Stan and Steve and asked him to take the tapes and put them in the mail. Stan and Steve knew each other through me but were very different and not really friends. On the tape to Stan, I said something like, "You should give Steve a chance. He's a little strange, but a really great guy."

Well, that sentence, which I had intended for Stan, I accidentally recorded on the wrong tape, and it went to Steve! Steve never forgave me. I tried to apologize but to no avail. A sad end to what should have been a lifelong friendship.

# CHAPTER 51

# I GET A NICKNAME

**My nickname is Gil. Here's how I got it. I was** in my junior year, living in Rieber Hall. The year was 1968. I had a small group of friends: Ken and Margie (they were dating), Barbara, Carol (who was my girlfriend), and Lorrie. We usually had our dinners together.

There's an interesting 2010 book by A. J. Jacobs called *My Life as an Experiment.* One of his experiments was to practice Radical Honesty for a month. For that month, he always had to give his true, unfiltered opinion. So, if his wife said, "Honey, what do you think of my new hairdo?" he had to tell her what he really thought. (You can imagine how dangerous that could be!) Well, Lorrie practiced Radical Honesty forty years before A. J. Jacobs tried his experiment.

So here we were standing in line waiting for the dining hall to open. On that day, I was especially happy. I had just bought some new sweaters and was wearing one of them. I think you can see what's coming. Lorrie turned to me and said, "That's the ugliest sweater I've ever seen." I don't remember my reaction, but luckily I wasn't practicing Radical Honesty. Now all of this is to explain that I had this group of friends and that one of them would give me my nickname.

I had to have an operation to remove a lump on the side of

my neck, and my friends came to visit me in the hospital. The doctor told me that the lump on my neck was in the area where, in fetal development, there's a gill-like structure that later disappears. The doctor jokingly said I had kept my gill. When I told them that story, Barbara said, "I now baptize you "Gilbert." I liked the name, and "Gil" became my nickname.

A few years later, I was living with some roommates in an apartment near UCLA. Someone called and asked for Steve. My roommate only knew me as Gil and said nobody by that name lived there. If I could do it over, I never would've taken a nickname. But I was a young college student, and when we are young, sometimes we do these kinds of things and years later wonder what in the world we were thinking. (Well, at least I didn't get a weird tattoo, like an eye on each cheek giving the appearance of having four eyes.)

When I was around seven, I would tease my brother, who was around four, calling him "Befery" (instead of Jeffery). He didn't think it was funny. Our mother would tell him to say, "Sticks and stones may break my bones, but names will never hurt me." He would say that, I would reply, "Beffery, Beffery, Beffery," and he would run crying to our mom. (This was before I was a Boy Scout, but I would have done it anyway.)

I don't have many other examples of nicknames. My sister, Maureen, was called "Mo." Sérgio called David "Neneca" because he was the baby (nenê) of the family. And to this day, David calls Paula "Vaca Leprosa" (leprous cow). This sounds strange, but my three kids are exceptionally close, are always joking and teasing each other, and nobody takes offense.

# CHAPTER 52

# MORE CALIFORNIA JOBS

**Between 1967 and 1971, I had a number of jobs.** During the summers of 1967 and 1968, I worked as an assistant programs director/organizer at a Los Angeles city school playground. During the summer break (June through August), the school playgrounds were open all day for the use of the neighborhood children. The city had a well-organized program for these playgrounds. There were two recreation supervisors for each playground, a director and an assistant. For each of those two summers, I was an assistant.

Our job was to organize recreational activities for the children. There would be games (tag, dodge ball, Simon says); sing-alongs (*This Old Man, She'll be Coming Around the Mountain, Row, Row, Row Your Boat);* and arts and crafts in which the children made things like necklaces, bracelets, masks, toilet-roll animals, etc.

Every Friday morning, we met for a training session in which we learned how to play the games, sing the songs, and do the arts and crafts projects that we would later do with the kids on the playground. There were around thirty of us. Try to imagine thirty 20-year-old college kids singing *This Old Man*, playing *Simon Says*, or dancing the *Hokey Pokey*. But the interesting thing is we all loved it. I think we had more fun in our training sessions than the young kids had with us on the playground.

When I wasn't playing with the young kids, I would sometimes write letters to my girlfriend, Donna, who had gone on vacation to Hawaii. Alas, that summer will also be remembered as "The summer I lost my girlfriend to a Hawaiian pineapple." When she came back, we broke up. Apparently she had been swept off her feet (or surfboard) by a Ukulele-playing, Mai Tai-drinking, blond, long-haired, California-born-and-raised surfer wearing an Aloha Hawaiian shirt who had gone to Hawaii to catch some waves and wound up catching something else.

In my first year of grad school (September 1969 to June 1970), I had a work-study grant to work as a language laboratory assistant in the UCLA Extension Program. In the evenings, I would assist teachers giving language classes. The teachers would bring their class to the lab, and I would put on the tape that they would like to use with their students.

I had one other work-study job. From September to December of 1971, I was a programs assistant at UCLA's International Student Center (ISC). My job was to help out at events. For example, every Friday afternoon the center hosted a "happy hour," in which there was a non-alcoholic punch as well as crackers and different kinds of cheeses. There were also cultural events related to different countries—a Brazilian carnival, for example.

One of the most shocking events in my life occurred during the time I was working at the center. It was a Friday evening around 10 p.m. I had just closed the door (which was of very thick transparent glass). There was a knock on the door. I saw two men standing in front of the door. I opened the door, and the following dialogue took place:

Men: We're from the police.
Me: (frightened) "How can I help you?"
Men: Do you know Sunny Dagowitz?
Me: No. Oh, yes. Wait. I was with her at a meeting here at the center earlier this afternoon.
Men: Well, she was murdered late this afternoon.

I didn't have any information that could be of help. I didn't know her. She was only an acquaintance who had participated in a meeting at the center earlier that day. As she was going to her car in one of the poorly-lit concrete parking structures, someone grabbed her from behind and stabbed her more than fifteen times. I can't remember any time in my life when I've been so shocked. And till today (2024), the case remains unsolved.

Finally, here are some celebrities and their jobs before they became famous: Jennifer Aniston (telemarketer); Barack Obama (ice cream scooper at Baskin Robbins); Kate Winslet (sandwich maker in a delicatessen); Tom Hanks (popcorn vendor); Michelle Pfeiffer (cashier at a supermarket); Whoopi Goldberg (morgue beautician); Chris Pratt (stripper); Harrison Ford (carpenter); Pierce Brosnan (professional fire eater). Sandra Bullock (bartender).

# CHAPTER 53

# CONFESSIONS OF A PSEUDO HIPPIE

**My pseudo-hippie phase began around 1970** and lasted until January of 1972, when I went to Brazil. I say "pseudo" because I wasn't exactly a hippie. Yes, I did have long hair (almost but not quite down to my shoulders). Yes, I did use a headband. And yes, I did dress in the typical hippie fashion of bellbottom pants and sandals. But there were no flower patches on my clothes, and I never wore clothing with psychedelic colors. I did have a full beard and a mustache (but so did Shakespear, Freud, Confucius, Plato, Hemmingway, Genghis Khan, Jesus, and, let's not forget, Santa Claus).

But I didn't do things associated with the hippie movement. I didn't do drugs. OK. I tried grass once or twice. The truth is, in the late 1960s and early 1970s, almost everyone smoked pot, at least once. In fact, you could walk out of your dorm room into the hallway and almost get high on the smell of grass coming from someone's room. So, two times hardly counts, and to be truthful (Boy Scouts don't lie), I don't even remember what it was like.

I protested against the war in Vietnam. Not because I really understood anything about why the United States was fighting that war. I didn't have the slightest idea. But I did know I didn't want to go.

And neither did any of my friends. In the student dorms, our evening "bull sessions" were always filled with discussions of how to avoid the draft. Suggestions included eating a couple dozen eggs to raise your cholesterol, kissing the induction officer—homosexuals weren't allowed in the army—and even cutting off your little finger. I joined the campus protests, chanting, "Hell, no. We won't go." I actually was called up and had to take a physical to determine if I was fit to serve. Luckily, I failed the physical. I don't remember why. (No, I didn't try eating twenty eggs the night before. And I still have both of my two little fingers.)

Shortly before I went to Brazil (January 2, 1972), I got a haircut and left my hippie appearance behind. I wasn't sure how I would be received looking as I did. Then one of the first teachers I met at the ICBEU was Evandro Ribeiro, whose hair was much longer than my hair had ever been and for which he was given the nickname "Evandro Beatle." As I said, I was never a true hippie, just a pseudo-hippie. But I do wish I had gone to Woodstock!

When I think of the sixties and the hippie movement, I think of my cousin Marlene Aron, who, sadly, died in 2018, at age seventy-five, hit by a car while crossing a street in San Francisco. Perhaps Marlene wouldn't have called herself a hippie, but she certainly was the embodiment of what the hippie movement was *supposed* to be: peace, love, tolerance, poetry, a better world.

She was a political activist (she marched in the civil rights and Vietnam anti-war protests); an accomplished artist (she has works on display in Youngstown's Butler Institute of American Art, the oldest museum of American art in the country); a poet;

and a free spirit who lived her life fearlessly and followed her own unique path unconcerned about what others thought she should do or be. She brings to mind the famous quote by Thoreau: "If a man does not keep pace with his companions, perhaps it's because he hears a different drummer. Let him step to the music which he hears, however measured or far away." And above all, she was a "gentle soul" who is sorely missed.

# PART SIX:

# BRAZIL

# (1972-2010)

# CHAPTER 54

# MY ROADS NOT TAKEN

**This is a reference to a poem by Robert Frost** (1874–1963). In this poem, a person walking along a path in a woods comes to a fork in the trail, takes one route, and comments that that decision made all the difference.

After I graduated from UCLA with a BA in Spanish in June of 1969, I was accepted to be a volunteer in the Peace Corps, a program established in 1961 by President John F. Kennedy (1917–1963) to aid developing countries. Volunteers receive a minimal monthly payment and do two years of community development. Famous Peace Corps volunteers include Reed Hastings (Netflix CEO); Paul Theroux (travel writer); Mae Jemison (NASA astronaut and first African-American woman to travel in space); and Lillian Carter (mother of President Jimmy Carter).

I would be going to Venezuela to do community development in a remote village. Training for that program was in a former nudist camp in the California town of Escondido (which in Spanish means "hidden"). Of course we looked for the nudists, but alas, they were no longer there.

Part of my training was learning how to raise chickens. Poor little chicks that never made it to "chickenhood." When they wanted me to learn to raise chickens, I began to wonder if that program was right for me. Then they sent me to a rural area (somewhere in Mexico), which consisted of a few houses and a school building, where I slept in a sweltering bed, hoping no spiders or scorpions would wish my company.

I came to the decision that that Peace Corps program wasn't for me, left the program, and enrolled in a master's in Spanish program at UCLA. My first road not taken took me away from Venezuela (where I probably would've met and married one of Hugo Chaves's nieces) and to graduate school at UCLA.

In addition to the courses for my master's degree in Spanish, I took some TESOL (teaching English as a second or foreign language) classes. One of my teachers told me about a US Information Service (USIS) program called English Teaching Fellow, a program for graduate students to teach English in binational centers. He encouraged me to apply, and I did.

On my application, I had to list four countries in order of preference. I don't remember what my first three choices were, but Brazil was my last choice. I received an offer to be an English Teaching Fellow in Peru. I was elated. I would take a break from my studies, spend a year in Peru, and come back speaking fluent Spanish. A perfect opportunity for a future Spanish teacher.

I wrote to Peru saying I would be thrilled to be an English Teaching Fellow at the Lima Peru-American binational center. But then something called Fate intervened. Two weeks later, I received an offer from the Brazilian-American binational center (ICBEU) in Manaus. Without hesitation, without even a second thought, I wrote to Peru saying I was no longer available and wrote to the ICBEU accepting the offer.

I mailed the two letters and then went to a UCLA library to look at a map of Brazil. I had never heard of Manaus, and I wanted to see where it was located. I looked at the map and said something like, "Holy Cow!" I actually said something stronger. But for this memoir, we'll leave it at Holy Cow. Manaus is located right in the middle of the Amazon Rainforest. There's no big city within five hundred miles.

Deciding to go to Brazil instead of Peru was my second Road Not Taken. Why would a future Spanish teacher go to Brazil and not Peru? I really don't know, but here are some things that possibly indirectly influenced that decision.

In the spring quarter of 1969, I had a beginning Portuguese class. My teacher was Dona Isabel Herwig. She had lived many years in Brazil, absolutely loved Brazil, and transmitted her enthusiasm in her classes. And this enthusiasm for Brazil passed on to me.

Then there was Brazilian music and the melodious sound of Brazilian Portuguese. One of the guys who lived on my dorm floor (Rieber Hall, 1969) gave me an audio tape of Sérgio Mendes, a Brazilian musician who had immigrated to the United States.

And my very first Carnival party, which wasn't in Brazil but was at UCLA's International Student Center in 1970 (and with a Mexican band playing Brazilian Carnival music!)

How much all of these things influenced my decision, I have no idea. Maybe I also liked the idea that there are no earthquakes in Brazil, especially in the Amazon region. Or maybe, as I would like to think, Fate had Neusa waiting for me.

# CHAPTER 55

# I SPEAK MY FIRST SENTENCE IN PORTUGUESE

**I arrived in Manaus on January 2nd of 1972 and** proudly spoke my first sentence in Portuguese on Brazilian soil. I remember exactly what I said. It wasn't a very long or complicated sentence. It had just ten words. But first, a few words about my travel to Manaus.

I spent my last night in the US at my dad's apartment. It was New Year's Eve, but I was too mentally exhausted to think of a New Year's celebration. My dad took me to the airport early in the morning of January 1, 1972. I flew to Mexico City, checked into my hotel, and spent the evening with the family I had stayed with in 1966. The next day I caught a Varig Airlines flight from Mexico City to Manaus. I arrived in Manaus around 5 p.m.

At that time, the only airport in Manaus was Ponta Pelada, which had only one runway and no tunnel from the airplane to the airport. I walked down the stairs onto the tarmac. My first impression: I felt like someone had dropped me into a sauna! It was overwhelmingly humid (I did get used to the humidity and reached a point where I no longer noticed it).

Then came customs and immigration. It was at customs that I spoke my first sentence in Portuguese in Brazil. Here's the exchange (translated): Customs agent: "Sir. Do you have anything to declare?" Me: Yes, I do. Customs agent: "What do you have to declare?" Me: "I declare that I am happy to be here in Brazil." To be clear, I understood what he meant, but I couldn't help making a little joke (but the sentence was true).

I was met at the airport by Professor Ruy Alencar, president of the Brazilian-American Cultural Institute (ICBEU). We got into his Ford Rural (a car that seemed half car and half tank), and he took me to the ICBEU, where there was a small studio apartment that would be my residence for the next two years.

The "I declare I'm happy to be here in Brazil" sentence spoken to the customs official was prophetic: I was in love with Manaus, Brazil, and the Brazilian people from the moment I arrived. For me, Manaus felt like a paradise. At that time, it had around 300,000 inhabitants (today it has over two million). But it didn't feel like a big, crowded, dangerous city: it felt small and welcoming. There was little traffic. I probably could've crossed Joaquim Nabuco (the street the ICBEU is on) with my eyes closed and not been hit by a car. Today, you have a long wait to cross this street.

There was little crime. On the weekends, I would walk back to my apartment at one or two in the morning (after going to a dancing club) and not feel the least unsafe. You had all the amenities of a big modern city (hospitals, excellent doctors, supermarkets, drugstores, department stores, movie theaters, and a world-famous opera house, "Teatro Amazonas").

There were no malls (the first mall, Amazonas Shopping, was inaugurated in 1991), but there were several downtown "shopping streets." No cars were permitted on those streets, but they were quite crowded with people shopping, often for electronics because Manaus has a duty-free economic zone, and there were store after store of imported products (electronics, perfumes, etc.).

I usually had dinner at a small luncheonette on Eduardo Ribeiro (the main downtown street). But shortly after I arrived, my money ran out. (I was a student before I came, and I arrived with very little money and was too shy to mention this to Professor Ruy.) So, for the rest of the month, I would go to a little snack bar/ice cream parlor in the square in front of IEA (one of the city's principal public schools).

There my dinner would consist of inexpensive finger foods, such as "ovo coberto" (a dough-wrapped hardboiled egg); "coxinha" (a deep-fried dough resembling a chicken thigh filled with shredded chicken); "Quibe" (from the Arab diaspora community; a small, elongated cylinder of a fried mixture of bulgar wheat, ground beef, and spices); or "pão de queijo" (a small baked ball of tapioca mixed with cheese, lightly crunchy on the outside and soft and chewy on the inside).

Manaus was a big city that felt like a small city, and I loved it.

# CHAPTER 56

# PROFESSOR RUY AND THE ICBEU

Professor Ruy Alencar (1925–2001) was one of the most important of all the people who have been in or passed through my life. He was a visionary, an idealist, who dedicated his life to strengthening the cultural ties between Brazil and the United States, to offering the people of Manaus cultural programs and events related to both cultures, and to helping young people achieve their full potential.

To give just one example, Professor Ruy encouraged (and the ICBEU helped sponsor) Roberto Vieira to do his master's in urban planning at the University of Tennessee. When Roberto returned, he held positions as Secretary of Urban Planning for the State of Amazonas, Rector of the University of Amazonas, and Director of INPA (National Institute of Amazonian Research).

Thanks to Professor Ruy and the ICBEU, Roberto realized his full potential and made incalculable contributions to the city of Manaus and the State of Amazonas. And Roberto was just one of many who were encouraged and supported by Professor Ruy and the ICBEU. Referring to the air force pilots defending London in World War Two, Winston Churchill (1874–1965) famously said, "Never in the field of human conflict was so much owed by so many to so few." I would like to say, "So much is owed by so many to Professor Ruy."

In July of 1956, a small group of teachers, businessmen, and Bank of Brazil employees, led by Professor Ruy, founded the English-Speaking Club to practice their English. Two years later, on September 15, 1958, with the presence of the American ambassador to Brazil, the English-Speaking Club officially became a binational center, taking the name Instituto Cultural Brasil-Estados Unidos (ICBEU).

It began with fifty students, the first student being Manoel Gonzáles y Gonzáles, a Spaniard from Madrid who was a Brazilian in his heart (as I am), a truly beautiful soul, and a practitioner of yoga (spiritual and physical), who until his death in 2006 at the age of eighty-eight gave yoga classes.

On July 4, 1969, with the help of a grant from the American Embassy, the ICBEU inaugurated its own building on Joaquim Nabuco Avenue. It was a three-story building with ten air-conditioned classrooms, a small library, a small language laboratory, an auditorium, and a teachers room/administration room. Behind the main building was a studio apartment for visiting teachers. That studio apartment would be my living quarters for my first two years in Brazil (1972 and 1973).

When I arrived in 1972, the ICBEU had only a handful of teachers: Lenise Barbosa, Dilma Dantas, Isa Akel, Sara Foinquinhos, Angela Penaforte, Evandro Ribeiro, Edilberto Pontes, Jorge Vasques, Ramiro Moreira, and Manuel Ribeiro, a future mayor of Manaus. Vera Caminha was the librarian (later it was Maria José). Ricardo Bianco was responsible for the audio-visual equipment (and for my cultural adaptation!). Today (2024), the ICBEU has 60 teachers and 4,000 students.

Its modern library of over 15,000 books is the best source for English language books in Manaus (and, in fact, in the Amazon region).

The ICBEU has a modern art gallery (under the direction of Ruth Alencar Peixoto, Professor Ruy's daughter) that has frequent showings of local artists. It also has an Education USA office where those interested can find information about studying in the United States. This office is headed by Isa Akel and Soraya Moresi.

You can't speak about the ICBEU without mentioning Helena Gomes da Silva (1928–2003), affectionately known as "Miss Helena," the stern and competent administrative secretary. I mean stern in a good sense. Miss Helen was the one who made sure everything was running smoothly. It was no small task to schedule the classes, handle the registration, and control the payments from the students and the payments to the teachers and staff. This was long before computers were invented, and everything was done by hand. Any teacher who dared to miss a class or come late for a class (unless he or she was either dead or in the hospital) received an earful. I can't think of anyone else who could've done the job nearly as well as she did. ICBEU's success owes a lot to Miss Helena.

# CHAPTER 57

# I LEARN PORTUGUESE

**Before I went to Brazil, I had a fair command** of Spanish. Spanish and Portuguese are quite similar, so to some degree my previous experience with Spanish was helpful. Also, I had studied one quarter of elementary Portuguese. (UCLA is on the quarter system. Each quarter has ten weeks.) But ten weeks isn't enough to make a difference. So, I arrived with little ability to understand and limited ability to speak.

I really wanted to become proficient in Portuguese and to become assimilated into the Brazilian culture and way of life. Not to stop being an American, but to be part of both cultures. I identified with Brazil, the Brazilian people, and the Brazilian culture. That (and the fact that I married a Brazilian) helped me in my effort to learn Portuguese.

Some people have a talent for learning languages. For them, learning another language is "as easy as pie." For example, my lifelong friend Stan Levinson can speak and read well in Spanish, Portuguese, French, Italian, German, Dutch, and Danish. He's fair in Thai and above beginner in Chinese, Japanese, Hebrew, Arabic, and Greek. Now, that's a talent for languages! I truthfully don't possess that talent. For me, learning Portuguese wasn't "as easy as pie."

My classes were always given almost 100% in English.

But after class, I tried to speak only in Portuguese. One of my evening students took great pleasure in correcting my Portuguese. I think it was almost her "life's mission." She would correct me, and I would feel a little sad. That resulted in my speaking a little worse. Which led to another correction, which made me feel even worse, and so on. Finally, I had to ask her to stop correcting me.

Sometimes after my last evening class I would go out for a beer with my friend Ricardo Bianco (who, as you might remember, was "responsible for my cultural adaptation"). We would go to Alex's Bar. (That was its name, but it was just a corner store with some tables outside where you could sit and drink a beer, or in my case a Guaraná—the native Brazilian soft drink.) One evening it was me, Ricardo, and someone else. After half an hour of listening to them speak in Portuguese and understanding very little, I said, "I need to go back to my apartment. My brain's fried from trying so hard to understand Portuguese."

Another incident also occurred with Ricardo at Alex's Bar. A shoeshine kid, probably ten years old, asked to shine our shoes. He looked at me and asked (in Portuguese) where I was from. I responded (in badly spoken Portuguese) "I'm Brazilian," to which he responded (in Portuguese) "You're not Brazilian, neither here nor in China."

For me, the most difficult sound to pronounce was LH, a sound we don't have in English. I would hold a mirror up in front of my face and try to pronounce the word "bacalhau" ("codfish"). I would make all kinds of contortions with my mouth and tongue but could never get it right. Codfish is a typical dish from Portugal that's common in Brazil. At first, I didn't like it. Maybe I didn't like it because I couldn't pronounce it! (Freud can explain this.)

Now, if you use the wrong word, it can sometimes be funny or even embarrassing. Once in my first year, there was a social event for the ICBEU's teachers and board of directors. One of the teachers, Evando "Beatle," was telling jokes. His jokes were funny, but you wouldn't want to tell them to your priest or rabbi. I decided to try my hand, translating a joke from English to Portuguese. You have to picture the situation. Not just the ICBEU teachers (all of whom were my age), but also the directors and their wives. Definitely a more formal group. I don't remember what my joke was, but it had the word "whorehouse." I didn't know that this word in Portuguese is much stronger than the word in English. When I said that word, everyone roared with laughter, not at my joke but at my gaffe. I didn't even get to finish the joke; the joke became the word I had spoken.

Then there was the time I asked a student if she was a chicken, meaning was she afraid to speak. My attempt at humor didn't go over very well. I didn't know that Chicken is a Brazilian slang expression for "slut." OOPS!

All of this reminds me of something that happened to a Brazilian high school exchange student in the United States. For the most part, students in Brazil learn American English. But she had learned British English, and that's what caused the problem. She needed an eraser and, in a loud voice, asked the class, "Does anybody have a rubber?"

# CHAPTER 58

# TWO SPECIAL FRIENDS

**I felt very comfortable in Manaus right from my** very first day. Everyone made me feel welcome. Brazilians are very hospitable, affable, friendly, and welcoming. But two people were particularly important for my adjustment to my new life in Brazil: Lenise Barbosa and Ricardo Bianco.

Lenise and I were colleagues at the ICBEU and later at the Federal University of Amazonas (UFAM), where we were both teachers in the Department of Foreign Languages and Literatures (DLLE). Lenise and her husband, Heráclio, were always explaining how things worked in Brazil and in Manaus in particular.

Manaus is a river city, a metropolis in the heart of the Amazon Rainforest, located near the confluence of the Negro and the Amazon rivers. So, naturally, fish is a major part of the diet. My first fish meal was with Lenise and Heráclio. Not long after I arrived in Manaus, they took me out to lunch and ordered a typical regional fish (carauaçu). Heráclio then said (in Portuguese) "Now I'm going to show this gringo how to remove the tiny fish bones." Only two people jokingly called me gringo: Heráclio and Ricardo. While this word usually has a pejorative sense, meaning "foreigner or outsider," they both used it as an affectionate term of friendship.

Lenise and Heráclio took me to my first carnival party in Manaus. The only thing I remember from that night (the party went until about 3 a.m.) was that the music from the band was so loud we couldn't hear each other talk, and everyone was in wild euphoric spirits. Lenise and Herácleo were also the architects of my "surprise" engagement (I didn't know I was getting engaged. More about that in a later story.)

Sadly, in 1981, Heráclio died in a tragic accident. He was an agronomist and had some land outside the city. On that tragic day, while he was talking with some of his workers, a tree fell on him. Some years later, Lenise managed to remake her life and married Karson Druckamiller, a good-humored, affable American from Texas.

When I met Ricardo, he was in charge of the audio-visual equipment at the ICBEU. Ricardo was twenty, and I was twenty-four. He spoke excellent English, so there were no communication problems. I lived in a studio apartment behind the main building of the ICBEU, and Ricardo lived a couple of blocks away. On Sundays, he would often show up and say, "Let's go. You're going to have lunch with us."

I obviously didn't look (or sound) like a Brazilian from Manaus. The skin color of people in Manaus is a beautiful tone, a mixture varying from light to fairly dark. I never really thought about skin color, but there were two amusing incidents that made me think I might "stick out like a sore thumb."

The first time I went to Ricardo's house, he introduced me to his sister, Maura, who was seventeen at the time. She looked at me and said (in Portuguese) "The Omo Total man has arrived." Omo Total is a laundry detergent that consists of a very white powder. The second funny incident occurred at a "balneário" (a kind of water place where people go to relax). I was lying on the sand. A young kid pointed to me and asked Mário Belem, the vice president of the ICBEU (in Portuguese), "What make/brand of man is that?"

When he wasn't inviting me to his house for Sunday lunch, Ricardo was inviting me to go swimming with him at Bosque Club or on the weekends in the evening to go out "chasing girls," though most of the time, we were just "standing on the corner watching all the girls go by" (like in that song from the 1956 Broadway musical, *The Most Happy Fella)*. Of one thing I am certain: Ricardo took his responsibility for my cultural adaptation very serious.

Ricardo was and is a true friend, a friend who is always there for you—a friend you can depend on. Steven J. Daniels (author of *Weeds in the Garden of Love*) said, "A good friend will help you move. But a best friend will help you move a dead body." Ricardo was that kind of best friend! (So far, I haven't needed that kind of help. But if one day I do, it's good to know I have a best friend I can depend upon.)

# CHAPTER 59

# MORE MANAUS FRIENDS

Jorge Vasques was a teacher at the ICBEU. In 1972, his family was the owner of the foremost hotel (Hotel Amazonas) and travel agency (Selvatur) in Manaus. Jorge offered to trade me three jungle tours for the translation of one of their tour flyers. I certainly got the better deal. I'm not a good translator. I did a number of translations over the years and can affirm two things: I'm not a good translator, and I hate translating. Which brings me to the *real* reason I try to be a good person: I'm afraid if I die and go to hell, my punishment will be to spend eternity doing translations.

Jesus Leong was born in the Philippines and came to Manaus in 1965. For a short time, he was a colleague in the foreign language department (DLLE). He would always smoke a cigar at the department meetings, leaving the room with a strong pungent aroma. (I thought it was a pleasant aroma, but I think I was the only one with that opinion.) In 1977, Leong left the university and, with a partner, opened two movie theaters.

Daniel Chaves, one of the founders of the ICBEU, was also a teacher in the department when I entered in 1974. Two years later, he retired to work full-time at the Bank of London (a branch in Manaus). Somehow I had managed to make a mess of my finances and needed a bank load, which Daniel arranged for me. He cosigned my loan (now that's a friend!). Every month I would take out a loan, use most of my salary to pay it back, and then need to take out another loan to get through the month until the next paycheck and the next loan. This cycle continued for about six months.

Brazilian workers in the federal sector receive twelve monthly salary deposits and a thirteenth paid half in July and half in December. That extra half-month's salary enabled me to pay off the loan without taking out another loan. When Neusa and I left Manaus in 2010, I hadn't had any contact with Daniel for some time, and sadly, I later learned he had died from COVID.

I met Waldir Rosas when he took an evening English class I was teaching (around 1975). Years later (1982), Waldir and his wife, Silvana, bought a condominium in the São José do Rio Negro apartment complex on Paraíba Street. Neusa and I had also just bought a condominium in that complex. It turned out that we were neighbors; our apartments were side by side at the top of a flight of stairs. At the time, Waldir was a well-known public prosecutor. That meant there were a lot of people who weren't exactly filled with love for him. I felt like putting a sign on my door that said, "O promotor mora ao lado" (the prosecutor lives next door).

Neusa and I sold our condominium and lost contact with Waldir and Silvana. In 2003, we reconnected again and would often go out to dinner together. I was retired and would sometimes visit Waldir at his law office to have a short chat. His cousin ran the office. I would say (in Portuguese), "If Waldir is busy, I'll come back some other time." His cousin would come back from Waldir's room and say, "Go on in. He said he's never too busy for Gil." Sadly, in 2017 I received a message from his daughter, Ana Silvia, saying that he had just passed away due to a heart attack. One of my dearest friends.

In 1977, I was designated to give the English component for a new master's program at INPA, the National Institute of Amazonian Research. Eduardo Lleras was the coordinator of the master's program in botany. He married one of his students, and the four of us (me and Neusa; Eduardo and Angela) would often go out for pizza together or eat a meal at one of our houses.

In one of our get-togethers, Eduardo said something about how he liked to view stressful situations (and everyone has stressful situations, unless you're living in a cemetery where everybody quietly minds their own business). He said, "I try to look at things as though it's ten years in the future, and I'm looking back." Good advice, but sometimes hard to follow in the heat of the moment. But, as I look back at some of the stressful situations I've had over my life, I can see his point. With the exception of my loss of Neusa, I can look back and even smile at almost everything that years ago upset me.

We two couples eventually drifted apart, and in 2006, after many years of no contact, I spoke with Eduardo. Sadly, it was to offer him condolences. A private business jet had collided with a GOL Airlines flight on route from Manaus to Brasília. All 154 passengers and crew members perished, among them Eduardo's wife, son, and grandson. An unthinkable tragedy.

# CHAPTER 60

# I MEET NEUSA

It was the beginning of November (1972), and in a month I would be returning to the States. I was walking down the street, lost in my thoughts, when I heard someone shouting. I turned around and saw this beautiful olive-skin girl approaching me, saying, "Ei, Americano. Ei Bonitão. Espera. Quero te conhecer." (Hey, American. Hey good-looking. Wait a minute. I want to know you.")

Of course, that's not how it happened. But I did tell this story a few times (always with Neusa present). I don't know why, but she never found it amusing. So here's how it really happened. It was a Sunday evening. *Fiddler on the Roof* was playing in a local movie theater. The movie started around 7 p.m. I decided to go because I had some time to kill.

Every Saturday and Sunday evening I would go to the two dancing clubs (Bancrevia and Cheik) located on Getúlio Vargas, a few blocks from my apartment. The clubs opened their doors at around 10 p.m. and closed around 2 a.m. Parties start later in Brazil. It seems that when a party in the United States is winding down, a party in Brazil is only about to begin.

The bands were very good. There was an electric feeling in the air. Warm balmy evenings, big crowds, everyone well-dressed (Brazilians are sharp dressers), everyone ready to dance and have a good time. So, that evening I went to a movie before going out to the dancing clubs. In the lobby, by chance, was Dona Tereza Assayag, one of my students from the ICBEU. She was with her two daughters, Mônica and Cinthya. Also with them was Neusa.

Dona Tereza introduced me to Neusa (and I sat next to her in the movie). After the movie was over, I said something that, in retrospect, is hard to believe I really said. I said (in Portuguese): "If you want to see me, I live at the ICBEU." (I still can't believe I actually said that, but I did.) Well, I waited. And I waited. And I waited.

She never came, so finally, I asked Dona Tereza for her number. She said she would first have to ask Neusa if she wanted me to call her. She did, and Dona Tereza gave me her number. I dialed it, and her brother João answered the phone. Here's the translated conversation: Is Neúúússa there?" (badly mispronouncing her name). Her brother: "No Neúúússa lives here," and he hung up. That same conversation occurred two or three times until I asked someone to make the call for me. I finally got through and was able to set a time to go to Neusa's house. From that moment on until I left to go back to the States about one month later, we were inseparable.

Lenise lived a few blocks from Neusa's parents' house. She made a goodbye lunch for me, and when I showed up alone, she asked where Neusa was. I said I didn't know she was invited. Lenise replied she assumed I would bring Neusa. So I went to her house and brought her to the lunch.

Which reminds me of the story about the American humorist Will Rogers (1879–1935). A Hollywood director invited Will to a party, and he showed up with a very voluptuous date. The director said, "Will, you didn't tell me you were bringing someone. Will responded, "But I did tell you. I said I would come with pleasure, and (pointing to his date) this is pleasure!"

Both Neusa and I had another "romantic interest" in our lives, which we conveniently (and thankfully) didn't mention to each other. She had a romantic interest in Rio de Janeiro, and I had a (kind of) romantic interest in Philadelphia. When I got back to the States (December 1972), I flew to Philadelphia, spent a few days with her, and knew Neusa was the one for me. And while I was gone, Neusa broke up with the guy from Rio.

So, I went back to Manaus. I flew from LA to Mexico City and checked into a hotel. The next morning, when I went to the airport to catch my Varig Airlines flight to Manaus, the attendant at the check-in counter said, "But your flight left yesterday, and the next flight is next week!" I don't know how I made that mistake. Well, Varig found a solution. They put me on a flight to Miami. From there, I was on a fight to Jamaica. From there, a flight to Georgetown, Guyana. Then a flight to Boa Vista (not far from the border of Venezuela). And finally, a flight to Manaus. PHEW! A long and tiring return.

Of course, the first thing I did was to go to Neusa's house. One last thing. My time at the Georgetown airport wasn't without an interesting incident. In the waiting room, two women from Georgetown were engaged in a conversation. Since I couldn't understand a word they were saying, I turned to them and said, "Excuse me. What language are you speaking?" One of them answered, "Why, it's English, of course" (spoken with a distinctly British accent).

# CHAPTER 61

# ENGAGEMENT AND MARRIAGE

**Nobody told me I was getting engaged! You would** think I would've been consulted. But I wasn't. It was June of 1973. It was evening, and me and Neusa, and Lenise and Heráclio were in my apartment in back of the ICBEU. Also present was Bruce Abrahamson, a friend from California who had come to visit me in Brazil.

I thought we had gone to my apartment to make plans for the evening. We were thinking of going to the Manaus river beach, Ponta Negra. But Lenise and Heráclio had something else in mind. Lenise turned to me and (in Portuguese) said, "Gil, I have something important to tell you. Here in Brazil, if you go out with a girl more than three times, it means you're in a serious relationship and that you're thinking of getting married."

I don't remember what I said or if Neusa said anything. Then Lenise continued, "So, to help you, we bought you and Neusa your wedding bands." In Brazil, when you get engaged, you use your wedding band on the right hand, and it goes on the left hand when you get married. Also, there's no diamond engagement ring for the fiancée. (A good reason for a man to marry a Brazilian. You start out saving money.)

She then gave a wedding band to me and another to Neusa.

All of this took place in Portuguese. Bruce looked at me and said, "I didn't understand a word that was spoken, but it looks to me like you're hooked." Then we all went to Ponta Negra Beach, where I did propose. Only later did Lenise tell me that the wedding bands were hers and Heráclio's. (I should've kept them and saved me some money.)

On Brazilian Valentine's Day (June 12th), I asked Neusa's father for Neusa's hand (and, of course, all the rest of her) in marriage. You can imagine how nervous I was. Doing that would've been hard in English; imagine in Portuguese.

Afterwards, we went to Chapeu de Palha (Straw Hat), a restaurant that was famous for its regional dishes (especially river fish, such as tambaqui, tucunaré, and pirarucu) and for its iconic design inspired by the straw hat Amazonian riverside dwellers use to protect themselves from the sun. It was an outdoor restaurant (there was no air-conditioned indoor dining), so it really was like sitting under a huge thatched, straw hat. Sadly, Chapeu de Palha no longer exists. Where it used to be there is now a gas station.

Speaking in Portuguese, I said to Neusa, "But your father didn't say much." She replied, "You spoke so much and didn't even give him an opportunity to speak." Some weeks later, we had a real engagement party at her parents' house. Now fast-forward to January 16, 1974, the day we got married. Since I'm Jewish, Neusa couldn't have a church wedding. So, we got married in the auditorium of the ICBEU. The wedding was in the morning. Part of the wedding ceremony consisted of readings of passages from *The Prophet* by Lebanese-American writer and poet Kahlil Gibran (1883–1931).

In the afternoon, we caught a flight to Bogotá. We spent a

few days in Bogotá and then took a train to Santa Marta on the Caribbean coast of Colombia. After a few days in Santa Marta, we went to Panama. It was our intention, and I am serious about this; it was our intention to go from Panama to Los Angeles by bus! But, luckily, I got a bad case of laryngitis and couldn't speak a word. So, we changed our plans and took a Pan Am flight to LA. Looking back, I don't know where my brain or head was to even think of going from Panama to LA by bus.

Neusa had always wanted a church wedding. In 2007, one of Neusa's cousins (Irmã Inês), who is a nun, arranged for a priest to conduct a Catholic service in the chapel of Colégio Auxiliadora (the Catholic school half a block down the street from our house). Thus, Neusa finally got her wish.

# CHAPTER 62

# NEUSINHA

I would usually refer to or address Neusa as Neusinha. In Portuguese, the suffix inho/inha forms a diminutive that expresses smallness (livrinho is a small book). But often it's used to express fondness and affection.

Neusa was calm and soft-spoken. She was known for her sweetness and gentle demeanor. But at the same time, she was strong-willed and had an iron-strong personality. She took her decisions and stood by them. When our first child, Paula, was born (1977), she decided to leave her university law course to take care of Paula (and later Sérgio and David). All three of our kids are doing well today, and in no small part that is due to Neusa. But the world has changed, and today that choice would be more difficult, often unfeasible.

After they became adults, one by one, our kids moved to Seattle, where my sister was living. It was hard, so very hard, for Neusa to see our kids move so far away. But never once did she try to discourage them. She faced our kids moving to the States with the same tranquility that a few years later would characterize her fight for her life against cancer. She knew that they would have more opportunities there than they would have in Brazil (sad, but true), so she put their future well-being ahead of her desires to have them close.

In July of 2010, we followed our kids and moved to Seattle, and in January of 2011, Neusa was hospitalized and diagnosed with cancer. When she received the news, she looked at the doctor and calmly said, "Ok. So, when are you going to cut it out?" Never once, from the time she was diagnosed until the day she passed away (October 9th), did she utter a single word of complaint. Never an angry word. Never once did she ask, "Why me?"

Even during her five hospitalizations brought on by acute and potentially fatal septic infections, she was always in good spirits. And when the doctors asked her how much her pain was on a scale of zero (no pain) to ten (the pain is out of control), she always responded one or two. She was a doctor's or nurse's dream patient, a patient who was always pleasant, always smiling, always optimistic. Even when the oncologist told her that the chemo treatments would stop because they weren't working, she was calm (while me and our kids were devastated).

Neusa was religious but didn't go to church on a regular basis. Nevertheless, I would classify her as a devout Catholic. When she was seventeen, she entered a convent to become a nun. She only left it because her mother had come down with hepatitis and went to Rio de Janeiro for treatment, and she was needed at home to help her father take care of her two younger brothers. Perhaps her time in the convent and her Catholic upbringing gave her the spiritual strength to face her cancer so calmly, so gracefully, so courageously.

Yes, Neusa was courageous and fearless. She wanted a cat, but since she was having terrible infections that were only controlled by special antibiotics, I was against it; I was afraid a cat scratch could lead to an infection. That worry didn't even enter her mind. We held a family meeting and took a vote. I was outvoted (our family is democratic, but I always have the minority vote) and jokingly given the nickname of "Pinochet" (the Chilean dictator) because I wished to be so controlling. Of course, all of my controlling was related to anything I perceived as a threat to Neusa's health.

There was a second time I was outvoted (and again called "Pinochet"). Neusa and the kids wanted to go to Hawaii. I was worried and was against it. Neusa wasn't the least bit worried. Well, we went, everything went smoothly, and it was a memorable vacation.

In Manaus, we always had a maid. One day my nephew Julio ran into our last maid at a bus stop. When he told her that Neusa had died, she broke into tears. I think it's a testament to Neusa's character that our former maid would be so affected, so saddened, by her passing.

Many years ago, on one of my trips back to the States, my brother and I were talking. He said we had both beaten the odds. We were both happily married when the odds were against a marriage succeeding (in the United States, between one third and one half of all first-time marriages end in divorce). He then went on to say that he knew the secret for a happy marriage: the man should give in to his wife's wishes 80% of the time and get his way 20% of the time. I agreed and even used that in my wedding speech at Sérgio's wedding (2013) and a second time at David's (2016).

Some say marriage is a lottery. Considering the number of marriages that end in divorce, maybe that's a good metaphor. But if marriage is a lottery, then I most certainly won the lottery.

CHAPTER 63

# MARRIAGE IS A PACKAGE DEAL

**Marriage is a package deal that includes your** in-laws. Maybe that's what prompted comedian/actor/writer George Burns (1896–1996) to say, "Happiness is having a large, loving, caring, close-knit family in another city."

I was lucky. Very lucky. I truly liked everyone in my "package deal." My "package deal" included Neusa's parents, her two brothers (João Luiz and César Augusto), as well as a half-brother and a half-sister (Isaias Junior and Ana Lúcia). It also included two sisters-in-law (Luzia and Angélica) and nieces and nephews.

Neusa's father (Isaias Profeta de Alencar Neto, 1921–2009) was an elegant, simple, unpretentious man. He was very handsome, so much so that when my mother first saw a picture of him, she said, "He looks like an Ethiopian prince!" And he did. He was an honest man, an incorruptible man. He was one of the chief government customs inspectors for Manaus. All the biggest companies depended on his signature for the items they needed to import. A dishonest person in his position could easily have enriched himself and bought a mansion. But not my father-in-law: he had a modest house in a middle-class/lower-middle-class neighborhood.

He was an expert mathematician (as was his brother Aristóteles), and he gave free (yes, free!) math tutorials to whoever needed help, either for school or in preparation for public exams for government jobs. Every evening his living room would be packed with his "tutees." Many benefitted from this generous act. Countless people in Manaus passed those public exams and were able to get good jobs (often in the public sector), thanks in part to the free tutoring of my father-in-law.

Which reminds me of when I went to get my driver's license. When I got in the car to take the driving test, the examiner looked at me and said, "How's your father-in-law?" I then knew I had passed, unless I did something seriously wrong, like running over a pedestrian.

In his later years, my father-in-law was completely blind. But, somehow, he found the inner strength to accept his blindness and found happiness in listening to the radio and chatting with family.

My mother-in-law (Neusa Lira de Alencar, 1923–2007) was small of stature but so big of heart. Every married man should have a mother-in-law like mine. Always with a smile on her face. I never heard her say a bad word about anyone. She only saw the good in people.

We lived a ten-minute walk from my mother-in-law's. Every day, between three and four in the afternoon, she would walk over to our house and have dinner with us. Then, after the evening "novela" (soap opera), we would walk her back to her house and spend an hour there talking with my father-in-law. This routine continued every day for over thirty years. And it was a real pleasure. In the final years of her life, when she could no longer walk to our house, we had a taxi pick her up and bring her.

As an aside, I loved the Brazilian "novelas." I don't think

"soap opera" is the best translation. The "novelas" are mini-series that run six days a week (Monday to Saturday) for around eight months. There's always a little drama and a very nice mix of humor. They're very well done; very entertaining. And it's so easy to become "hooked" on them. I know. I was. Once, when all three of our kids were in the States, one of them called in the middle of "my novela." I said I couldn't talk and asked them to call back later!

Whenever I got sick with a small cold, my mother-in-law would say (in Portuguese), "Don't worry. A bad vase doesn't break." It brings a smile to my face just remembering her saying that. When he was little, my son Sérgio was "a handful" (to say the least!). Whenever he was misbehaving (which was often), my mother-in-law would grab her rosary and tell him she was going to pray to the lost souls in Purgatory for him, and he would immediately calm down.

I'd like to rephrase the quote from George Burns that I began with: "Happiness is having a father-in-law and a mother-in-law like the ones I had the privilege of having."

# CHAPTER 64

# MARRIAGE IS A PACKAGE DEAL (CONTINUED)

**In early 1973, Neusa and I were dating. Saturday** mornings I would usually have breakfast at a little luncheonette, which had the unlikely name of "Go-Go." Other than the name, there was nothing erotic about this eatery. There were no sexy, scantily clad, dancing waitresses. After breakfast, which usually consisted of a toasted French bread roll and coffee, I would go over to Neusa's (and have another breakfast).

One day before going to Neusa's, I saw what seemed to be something strange happening in the middle of the street, which that day was blocked for cars. There was a long line of teenage schoolgirls waiting to take their picture with a young, long-haired guy, who, when I got closer, turned out to be my future brother-in-law, João Luis. He could've given Cassanova (1725–1798) a run for his money.

Some years later, João worked as a photographer, filming weddings and other events. He didn't have a car so he would lug all of his heavy equipment on the bus. In the last years of his father's life, when his father was an invalid, João would get up every morning at 3 a.m. and carry his father into the bathroom for him to take a shower. Every single morning at 3 a.m.! Looking back, I confess João never received the recognition he deserved. And, sadly, João is no longer here; he died in 2012, a few months after Neusa.

When I think of my brother-in-law César Augusto, two things immediately come to my mind: Carnival and food. Every year, he would put on his colorful Carnival costume and join the Carnival celebrations. I can still see his wide ear-to-ear grin of pure enjoyment.

Brazilian Carnival has been called "the greatest party on earth." And that's not an exaggeration. Carnival parades are characterized by strong percussion; elaborate, colorful, luxurious costumes; extravagantly decorated floats; and sensual dancing.

My first year in Manaus (1972), I went to a Carnival party held at a large club called "Olímpico." I arrived around eleven o'clock. By midnight, the club was packed, and I found myself almost pinned to the back wall. Shortly after that, I went back to my apartment behind the ICBEU. That was even more exciting than the Carnival party. At that time the ICBEU had a low wall in front of it, and I had to pull myself up over it and jump down. The exciting part was wondering if the 74-year-old nearly-blind night watchman would mistake me for an intruder and shoot me.

César loved to cook, was an excellent cook, and with his wife, Angelica, always helped his mother prepare the holiday meals. Eventually César and Angelica opened a small eatery in front of their house. They barbecued meat on a spit and served it with farofa (toasted cassava flour). Many people opened similar barbecue eateries. They were jokingly called "barbecue cat eateries." As far as I know, that was only a joke. (But you never know.) It took me a few years to get accustomed to "farofa." Today I love it, but at first it reminded me of sawdust.

For a few years, César worked as a monitor/aide at the Catholic school Nossa Senhora Auxiliadora. The students absolutely adored him. That experience led him to get a college degree in education. It was no easy task for him to start a college course at the age of forty, but he applied himself "with gusto" and earned his degree. Sadly, César died in 2011, a few months before Neusinha.

My brother-in-law Isaias Junior (named after his father) has been a graphic designer for over twenty years and is now the owner/manager of a barbershop. It's not an ordinary barbershop; it's a Beatles-themed barbershop, decorated with Beatles posters, where you can get a haircut and a shave while listening to Beatles music. My sister-in-law Ana Lúcia is a psychologist and is now starting a new career as a pharmacist. One more pharmacist in my family. My son-in-law, Thomas, is a pharmacist (and one of the hardest workers of anyone I know). If I had to describe Junior and Ana in one word, it would be "super-nice." They are two of the nicest people I know. There are certainly some people who are as nice; but there is nobody nicer.

My Brazilian extended family also includes nieces and nephews. João and Luzia's children are Carmem, Joãozinho, and Inês. César and Angélica's are Júlia Gabriela (my goddaughter), Júlio César, and Paulo José. The two families lived about five minutes from our house, so my kids and their cousins grew up together, just as I grew up with my cousins in Youngstown, Ohio. Cousins growing up together is truly a blessing.

# CHAPTER 65

# THE BEGINNING OF MY TEACHING CAREER

**My teaching career could be divided into four phases:**

- Graduate studies for a teaching credential: (UCLA, 1969-1970).

- ICBEU: 1972 to about 1978.

- UFAM: 1974 to 2003 (the year I retired).

- CT-PIM: a technology company. 2003 to 2010 (the year I left Brazil).

In the fall of 1969, I began a graduate-level program at UCLA leading to a State of California Standard Teaching Credential with a specialization in secondary teaching (Spanish and English). As part of the credential program, I had to do a semester of "student teaching" in a public school under the supervision of the class's regular teacher. I was assigned to teach Spanish in a high school not far from UCLA. This was in the spring of 1970. It was my first experience teaching.

My students were in the 9th grade, on average fifteen years old. I gave my classes "with gusto." Perhaps with a little too much "gusto." I had a long wooden pointer that I used to show the students what I wanted them to pay attention to. One day I wanted a student to repeat a word that was on the board. Touching it with my pointer, I quickly turned around, said, "And you," and pointed to a student, almost spearing him in the chest.

At the conclusion of my student teaching, the students surprised me with a going away gift, a book, which they had all signed with short messages to me. Here are two of their messages. From Randy: "From the greatest potential in the class to the greatest in the class." From Steve: "You're a great teacher. Keep swinging and keep cool, you cool cat!" But my favorite message was from Rolando:

> "I have often wondered, if you ever wondered
> what we wondered about you. In short, what we think.
> At first, a fire hydrant with epilepsy in the hand.
> A neurotic schizoid.
> But in all, we thought you were trying hard.
> When we found that you were, we lost all faith in you.
> Nevertheless, we like you. Thank you. Don't come back.
> No, you are always welcome."

When I came to Manaus in January of 1972, I had had no previous teaching experience other than my supervised student teaching. So, you could say I learned to teach at the ICBEU, and it couldn't have been at a better place. The teachers at the ICBEU were fluent in English and were all skilled classroom practitioners.

For several years, I gave teacher training courses to ICBEU teachers and others who wished to become an English teacher. I always gave those courses with Edilberto Pontes, a talented, funny, and creative teacher. Edilberto was from Fortaleza, the state capital of Ceará in northeastern Brazil. He would always entertain us by speaking English with a northeastern "caipira" (hillbilly) accent. Some years later, he opened his own English school.

Edilberto had very long hair. I was learning to develop pictures at the Aliança Francesa, a French language and cultural institute downtown not far from the ICBEU. I took a picture of Edilberto and a picture of Neusa's dog. In the photo lab at the Aliança Francesa, I transposed Edilberto's head onto the body of Neusa's dog and printed it out. I posted this picture on the bulletin board in the teachers' lounge. (which at that time was also the ICBEU's office). A young student walked into the office, saw the picture, and asked, "Que bicho é este?" (What creature is this?).

As I had just arrived in Brazil, my Portuguese was still limited. I had a group of teens. Brazilians have difficulty pronouncing the ING sound. I came up with a "brilliant" teaching technique. I would break the sound down into two sounds that the students could easily pronounce. Here's how I proceeded. Me: "Say *kah.*" (the class repeated). "Now, say *gah.*" (the class repeated). The problem came when I asked them to combine the sounds into what I thought was just a meaningless combination of the two sounds. Me: "Repeat, *kaga.*"

I had no idea that that was a word in Portuguese. All of those young teenagers repeated after me while giving me strange looks. After class, one of the older students came up to me and asked me if I knew the meaning of the word I had asked everyone to repeat. I said, "What word?" And then I remembered my Spanish. For those who don't know Spanish or Portuguese, "caga" means "He/she shits."

# CHAPTER 66

# UFAM

**In August of 1974, I began teaching at the** Federal University of Amazonas (UFAM). Founded in January of 1909, UFAM is the oldest university in Brazil. It's a public university. There's no tuition; the students study for free, but entrance is by a highly competitive exam called the "Vestibular."

When I began teaching at UFAM, the Institute of Humanities and Letters (ICHL) was in the old São José Seminary buildings on Emílio Moreira Street. The Department of Foreign Languages and Literatures (DLLE) had a single large room. My desk was at the very end of the room, next to a window. Outside the window was an enormous jackfruit tree.

Isabel Gomes da Silva, affectionately known as "Miss Isabel," was head of the department. Miss Isabel was one of the founders of the ICBEU and one of the pioneering English teachers in Manaus. She was a little short, a tiny woman, but very outspoken and never afraid to say what she wanted to say.

Some years later, when she was a little older, probably in her sixties, she came to a department meeting with a new hairdo: she had dyed her hair blue. She was truly ahead of her time. This was long before the younger generation began dyeing their hair unusual colors. (My granddaughter Isabella, age nineteen, has streaks of blue in her hair.)

One of the first subjects I was asked to teach was methodology for English teachers. For this course, every week I produced a mimeographed handout (yes, mimeographed). This was my first attempt at materials production, something that would occupy my time and energy throughout my career.

Besides the methodology course, I taught American literature, conversation, English grammar, cultures of the English-speaking world, and basic English for all courses, not just for English majors.

In 1978, I was designated to give the English component for a new master's program in biological sciences at INPA (National Institute of Amazonian Research). My class began at 7 a.m. As my friend Ângela Oliveira would often exclaim, "Ninguém merece!" (nobody deserves this). That's how I felt: nobody deserves a seven o'clock class. However, I really enjoyed working with those students and again produced my own materials.

In 1983, I once again had a 7 a.m. class (and would say to myself, Ninguém merece!). The class was a group of first-year law students. Among the twenty or so students was an older dignified man of about fifty years of age. He was calm, polite, and studious. Actively participated in all class activities. A model student. The kind of student every teacher desires. Looking at him and talking with him, you had the impression he was a kind, beloved grandfather. After he had missed a few classes, I asked one of the students, "What happened to Carlos? He replied, "Didn't you see it in the newspaper?" Me: "See what?" Student: "He was sent back to prison!" It turns out this kind, amiable, grandfatherly man two years earlier had killed his fourteen-year-old stepdaughter, for whom he had "unfatherly" desires.

We moved to the new campus in 1985. The campus is in an urban forest of 2.6 square miles, one of the largest urban forests in the world. The design of the campus and its buildings was the work of Severiano Mário Porto, the same architect who designed the Chapeu de Palha restaurant. The campus is unique: the buildings use natural materials and blend in perfectly with the surrounding urban forest.

I shared an office with Regina Marinho and Bruce Osborne. I met Regina when I first arrived in Manaus when she was a sixteen-year-old student in my first conversation class at the ICBEU (1972). Some years later, I sat on the examination board when she applied to become a teacher in our department. I distinctly remember how impressed I was with her presentation. Regina and Bruce later worked together to produce an innovative course linking literature and films based on literature.

As of today (January 2024), Bruce is still teaching at UFAM; in fact, he's been at UFAM so long that when he finally does retire, he'll "walk into the sunset" using a walker. ("Into the sunset" is an allusion to the cliched happy endings of the westerns on TV during the 1950s and the 1960s, in which the cowboy hero rides his horse into the sunset.)

I enjoyed my time in the department. The teachers were wonderful individuals. I can truly say that, without exception, I liked each and every one of them. I retired in 2003 and went to work teaching English at CT-PIM, a technology company. I taught there until we (me and Neusa) left Brazil in July of 2010.

I will end with a mention of everyone who at one time or another was part of my life in the Department of Foreign Languages and Literatures at the Federal University of Amazonas.

English teachers: Angela Penaforte, Bruce Osborne, Daniel Chaves, Dulce Alencar-Lake, Edlamar Benevides, Edith Corrêa, Gilma Batista, Irene Alves, Isabel Gomes da Silva, Isis Araújo, Jesus Leong, Lenise Barbosa, Lillian DePaula, Lúcia Joana, Marluce Portugaels, Marta Monteiro, Nelson Fontouro, Nilton Hitotuzi, Noemi Saraiva, Paulo Renan, Regina Marinho, Ruth Bork, and Sérgio Freire;

French teachers: Herbert Braga, Jacira Salazar, Jane Jatobá, João Luiz, Márcia Lira, Elisa Bessa, Milton Hatoum, Neide Ferreira, and Nereide Santiago.

Spanish teachers: Amélia Granados, Elsa Barria; German teacher: Marianne Schubart; and administrative staff: Kátia Santana, Erlen Dias, José Carlos, Lilian Nery, and Odette (couldn't find her last name).

# CHAPTER 67

# MY WORK WITH TPR

Total Physical Response (TPR) is a method for teaching languages developed by Dr. James J. Asher (1929–2022), a psychologist who taught at San José State University in California. In this method, the learners initially don't speak but first develop their ability to understand the spoken language by performing actions (called "commands"). Some examples: Walk to the door; Shake your head; Turn off the lights; Pull your hair. When the learners have absorbed a reasonable amount of the language, they give the commands to the teacher and their classmates.

Much of my professional career was devoted to developing teaching materials based on this method. My work with TPR owes itself to my colleague Marluce Portugaels, a fellow teacher, first at the ICBEU and later at the Federal University of Amazonas, and to my mother divorcing her second husband. Here's how it happened. The year was 1975. Marluce did a training course for EFL (English as a Foreign Language) teachers in San Diego, where she worked with a teacher who was using TPR. When she came back, she made a presentation for the teachers at the ICBEU. I was intrigued by her presentation.

Around 1977, my mother divorced her second husband.

So, what does that have to do with me and Total Physical Response? I'm glad you asked. Well, after the divorce, my mother moved from Los Angeles to Santa Clara, which is near San José, where Dr. Asher was teaching. That year, Neusa and I went to the States. We visited my mother, and I got in touch with Dr. Asher. We had a short talk in his office, and then he took me to the audio-visual center, where I viewed films he had made showing children and adults learning German, Spanish, French, and Japanese through TPR.

I was impressed. The theoretical premises in his published articles made sense, and the films showed that the learners achieved a good level of listening comprehension and could produce beginning-level speech without excessive hesitancy. But I needed to see how it would work with my students in Brazil.

Here's how my first experiment with TPR went: I had a beginning-level class. I asked the students to take out a sheet of paper. I then told them to make a paper ball. They were a little surprised but did as I had directed. I then gave the command, "Throw the paper ball at me." All of a sudden, I was bombarded by twenty paper balls. They loved it, and I felt there was something to this TPR business that needed to be investigated.

At the beginning of my work with TPR, I would bring props to class, such as a candle, a sponge, a doll, a toy truck, etc. The students would carry out commands using these objects, as for example, "Light the candle"; "Now blow it out." One day I brought my daughter to the university (not as a prop). She might've been four at the time. She looked behind my desk and saw the bag of props. She then exclaimed, "Papai, meus brinquedos!" (Daddy, my toys!).

I would use TPR for ten minutes every class. I had the students walk, jump, and hop, among other actions. The students were a little surprised at first, but they always responded positively. And they always got their "revenge." After two weeks, I turned the class over to them and said I would do anything they commanded, as long as it was in English. They kept me running, jumping, and hopping around the class for the full forty-five minutes (if I'd had a gym membership, I could've cancelled it!). There were also many silly actions they told me to perform, such as "Sit on the floor and quack like a duck." Everything was done in a spirit of fun.

Most of my colleagues in the department were skeptical. However, there was one important exception: Ruth Alice Bork. She also started using TPR as an extra activity in her classes and reported positive results. Her support and encouragement, along with the positive acceptance by my students, resulted in my deciding to experiment more with this method.

My next step (1978) was to make a film documenting my work with TPR. This film was made with the help of the Amazonas State Educational Television Station. They came several times to film my class and later helped me edit it into a forty-five-minute film. This film was important because it showed the kind of unhesitant connected speech that could be obtained by using TPR as the principal method with beginning-level university students who were not English language majors.

One memory from that group stands out. It was the first day of class. One of the students, Justina, who was a little older, around forty, and a little more formal in demeanor, arrived late. When she walked in the door, she saw me jumping around the class with five students jumping in a single file behind me. I can still see the look of astonishment on her face.

In 1984, I made another film with the help of two of my former students who were teaching in the Amazonas State school system, Sandra Campos and Rosa Muniz. The film, again made with the help of the Amazonas State Educational Television Station, showed fifth grade state school students learning English through TPR. Results similar to those obtained with my university students were obtained and documented.

From 2000 to 2003, my materials based on TPR were used in the state (SEDUC) and the municipal (SEMED) schools. In 2005, new administrations in the State and Municipal Secretariats of Education had a commission evaluate the materials, and different books were chosen. Nevertheless, I still contend that materials based on TPR are the best option for the Brazilian public schools, and perhaps I will make that point in a future article in a Brazilian academic journal.

# CHAPTER 68

# PUBLICATIONS, PRESENTATIONS, AND WEBSITES

**I'm going to speak a little about my professional** activities other than teaching. At the outset, let me state I'm not tooting my own horn. In reality, my professional output was quite meager. I only published ten articles in professional journals or conference annals, three of which were published *after* I retired and was living in the United States.

I want to begin by tipping my hat to three of my former students (and later colleagues at UFAM): Marta Monteiro, Sérgio Freire, and Nilton Hitotuzi. They each have innumerous publications in professional journals or conference annals (Nilton has nearly thirty), have published one or more books, have given presentations in a great many professional events throughout Brazil (each of them more than fifty), have supervised many students' research projects and master's theses, and have held positions of distinction within the university and beyond (Sérgio was Secretary of Education for the city of Manaus). They are the epitome of what it means to be a university professor. They have my recognition, esteem, and admiration.

My articles weren't research-oriented. They were practical

teacher/classroom-oriented, which of course doesn't make them less valuable. Here are four of them. "Games for the classroom and the English-speaking club" was published in 1982 in the *English Teaching Forum,* a publication of the US Department of State. "A practical guide to actions in the classroom" (*MEXTESOL Journal*, 2015) and "Drawing out language: Using drawings to develop listening and speaking" (*English Teaching Professional*, 2018) were both based on my work with Total Physical Response. "Enliven your class and engage your students with fun facts" (*English Teaching Forum,* 2023) is my most recent article (hopefully more to come).

Over the years, I made presentations in a small number (fifteen) of professional meetings or congresses, all in Brazil, with the exception of the *Twelfth Annual TESOL Convention* in Mexico City in 1978, where I gave a workshop, "Games for the Classroom and the English-Speaking Club," which became my 1982 *Forum* article.

Unfortunately, only four of my presentations were later published in the conference annals or as an article in a journal. I regret not having written up the other presentations and submitted them for publication.

I published two books (*Listen and Perform; The Command Book*) and one downloadable PDF file (*The Best Way to TPR any Grammatical Feature in English*) through Dr. Asher's publishing company, Sky Oaks Productions.

In 2000, through the University of Amazonas Press, I published *Point and Touch: Grammar and Vocabulary Exercises for Beginning EFL Students*. It's a "light" form of Total Physical Response in which the learner points to or touches a figure that illustrates the grammatical point or vocabular item in the sentence spoken by the teacher. For example, Touch the taller man; Point to the girl who is crying. That book later served as the basis for the materials I produced for the Amazonas State public schools. The illustrations were done by Joubert Lima (one of my daughter's college classmates), and whatever value the book has, much of that value is due to his superb artwork.

Since leaving Brazil in 2010, I've self-printed four books: Poems I have Enjoyed: A Personal Anthology (2012; an anthology of 214 poems from 101 poets); Listen and Draw: Easy Drawing Activities for the EFL/ESL Classroom: A Teacher's Resource Book (2015); More Poems I have Enjoyed (2015); and Fun Facts for the EFL/ESL Classroom: A Teacher's Resource Book (2021).

My work has also included two documentary films: *Total Physical Response: A Fun and Efficient Method* (1978) and *Total Physical Response in the Fifth Grade* (1984). With the help of a professional web designer (Axess Web Design), I've also produced two websites, one for learners (https://teacher--steve.wixsite.com/esl-station) and one for teachers (www.teachersteve.us). (In the future, this might become Teacher--steve.wixsite.com/teachersteve.)

While I wish I had produced more articles, I can honestly say that I feel that some of what I did produce was "pretty good" and of value to my intended audience (EFL teachers and teachers in training). And I'm not through producing. I still have a number of EFL teaching projects I hope to realize in the coming years.

# CHAPTER 69

# HOW NOT TO BE A GOOD TEACHER

The first two examples of how NOT to be a good teacher occurred early in my career. Flávio was my student in an elementary English class and had missed a lot of classes. Then, one of the students in the class, a friend of his, gave me a message: Flávio had pneumonia and asked that his absences be excused.

At that time, teachers had an attendance sheet. Missing too many classes resulted in flunking the course. The students had to have attended seventy percent of the classes; otherwise, "See you next semester."

At that time, I was a little (very?) rigid in my thinking. If you were absent, it was an absence on the attendance sheet; no exceptions, not even for the funeral of your dog or mother-in-law. So, I told the student to tell Flávio that I hoped he would be well soon, but I wouldn't be able to excuse his absences. Not long after that, Flávio returned to class and told me how upset he was for my lack of understanding.

And he was right. After that, I decided I would be more understanding, especially in cases of illness. I wouldn't flunk a student for missing classes, unless they missed almost all of the classes. But I would flunk a student for not achieving a passing grade.

Which brings me to Ana Ely. Ana was one of my first students. She was in the course English Teaching Methodology, around 1975, give or take a year. A passing grade was five. The grading system was one to ten. That means the grades on all of the tests had to average out to at least five. Ana's final average for the course was less than five, so I didn't hesitate to flunk her.

Ana was in her last semester before graduating, and my failing her meant that she missed graduating with her classmates. In a Brazilian university, you have most of your classes with the same classmates throughout the four years of your course. So, you really get to know your classmates. This results in strong friendships, and not graduating with them, not being able to celebrate together with them, would be incredibly sad and painful. This is what happened to Ana.

But it gets worse. I know. It's hard to imagine how this could get worse. But it does. Her grade point average was 4.9. So, she was flunked because of one decimal point! Of course, I never should've flunked her, especially for one decimal point. But she never once complained. She didn't come to my office and tell me her boyfriend was Mike Tyson (world heavyweight boxing champion from 1987–1990) and that he would be very upset if she didn't pass. She didn't threaten me with Macumba (Brazilian black magic). She took the course again and graduated the following semester.

Fast forward twenty years. I hadn't seen Ana since she had graduated. I was at the Amazonas Shopping Mall, in the anchor department store BEMOL. There in a line waiting to pay her carnê (booklet of installment payments) was Ana. I told her I was sorry I had flunked her and stopped her from graduating. She said it was okay and that it had been good for her to take the course again.

This last story is a little different. It occurred later in my career. I don't remember this student's name. Maybe Freud can explain why I don't remember her name, but if I did, I wouldn't put it to print. She was very fluent in English. On a scale of one to ten, her English was a ten.

She was in my Cultures of the English-Speaking World class. I assigned a composition. Her composition was excellent, well-developed, and without a single grammatical error. This wasn't surprising considering her outstanding command of English. But something didn't seem quite right. Her composition seemed like "déjà vu." Then I realized where I had seen it before, and I found the source from which she had copied it. So, I gave her back the composition, writing, "One point for you and nine points for the author!" I thought I was being clever, witty. But of course I was being an "ass." (Or should I say, a schmuck?)

I should've called her in, talked with her, and asked her why she felt the need to copy. I could've given her a second chance.

Luckily, there were only a few (as far as I know) of these "not good" teaching incidents.

# CHAPTER 70

# FIRST RESIDENCES

**My first residence in Manaus was a studio** apartment (provided by the ICBEU) in back of the main building. It was small but comfortable. It came with a small wardrobe, a charcoal water filter, and a two-burner electric hotplate.

Once a week, ICBEU's cleaning lady, Dona Amélia, would tidy up my apartment. Also, once a week a washerwoman would come and take my clothes, wash them in a creek near her house, and bring them back neatly folded and smelling good from whatever detergent she used.

I spent two years in that apartment. I lived alone, which I really enjoyed, but I did have two roommates for a few months. My first roommate was my sister, who came to stay with me from July to November of my first year (1972). My other roommate was Lenise's husband, Heráclio. That was in my second year (1973). Lenise was spending two months in Rio de Janeiro taking a course sponsored by the Fulbright Commission. So for those two months, Heráclio came to live with me.

Manaus is always hot, even in the evening, so people use their air conditioners all night long. However, I'm sensitive to the cold, so not long after we had both gone to bed, I would wake up feeling cold and turn off the air conditioner. About thirty minutes later, Heráclio would be feeling hot and would turn it back on. Then, a little later, I would turn it off. It seems we had this "dance" every night. In a way, it reminds me of the 1968 movie *The Odd Couple*, in which two divorced men (neurotic neat-freak Felix Unger and fun-loving slob Oscar Madison) decide to live together. Not that there's any resemblance between me and Heráclio to the film's two protagonists.

When Neusa and I returned to Brazil after I finished my master's at UCLA (July 1974), we stayed for about two weeks at her parents' house and then rented a one-bedroom house a few blocks away. Neusa's father bought us all the furnishings (bed, dresser, wardrobe, stove, refrigerator, sofa, etc.). The house was small but perfect for our needs.

Living so near Neusa's parents was convenient. More than convenient, it was a blessing. Every evening we would go there and spend an hour or so visiting with them. That became our norm and continued for thirty-five years, until we left Brazil in 2010. Also, Sundays we usually had lunch with Neusa's family (mother, father, two brothers). I really enjoyed those visits. I never once felt I was doing something just to please my wife.

Neusa's mother provided our lunch, which is the main meal in Brazil. Since she was cooking for her own family, we gave her money, and she made a little more food. Every day our maid would go to Neusa's mother's and pick up a "marmita" (a set of nesting round aluminum pans each containing part of the meal). There was always a pan of rice, beans, salad, farofa (toasted cassava), and meat, chicken, liver, or fish.

We decided that the interior of the house needed painting and that we would do it ourselves. My experience with painting was limited to two or three acrylic art paintings. The most you could say of them was that "they weren't bad." That certainly didn't prepare me for painting the inside walls of our house. But that didn't deter me. I don't remember what we did (I think we just tried to paint over the old paint without first preparing the surface), but after about two hours, we knew that our painting didn't even reach the level of "not bad." The next day we hired a professional house painter.

In January of 1977, when Neusa was seven months pregnant with Paula, we decided to move to a bigger house on "Travessa Rotary." It wasn't a good move. With Neusa heavily pregnant, it was too far for us to walk to her parents' house, so we went there less frequently and by taxi.

In June of 1979, we move to an apartment in a building near Colégio Auxiliadora, in front of the small square. It was a spacious two-bedroom apartment. There was no master bedroom, but there was a large, ceramic-tiled bathroom located off a hallway that ran between the two bedrooms. The living room was fairly long, carpeted, and had wood paneled walls, giving it a "classy" feel.

When we rented the place, I was surprised to find there were wires hanging from the ceiling in the living room but no light fixtures. The property management agency said that since most renters want their own decorative light fixtures, it was the policy to rent without the fixtures.

We stayed in that apartment until 1981, when we bought our first house. It was comfortable, it was cozy, and it was conveniently located near Neusa's parents house.

# CHAPTER 71

# MANAUENSE

In 1981, we bought our first house. It was in Conjunto Manauense, a housing development that had been around for a number of years. It was a nice, spacious house. But there were some problems we hadn't foreseen or weren't made aware of when we bought it, and thus we didn't remain in it for a long time.

The house was below street level. When we bought it, we didn't realize that that could be a problem, and a problem it was because the street had poor drainage. So when it rained hard (which was common in Manaus, located in the middle of the Amazon Rainforest), water could potentially pour from the flooded street down the driveway onto the front yard and into the house.

The couple that sold us the house had "forgotten" to mention that problem. But the day we moved in, the previous owner showed me a heavy rectangular metal plate about three feet tall and as long as the width of the driveway. It could be fitted into slots on either side of the driveway and thus effectively block water from entering. No water could enter via the front yard because it was protected by a low wall. Every morning before leaving for work, I had to remove the plate, drive my car out to the street, and then put the plate back in place. And repeat the process when I came home from work.

That wasn't a "pain in the neck." It was a pain in the "gluteus maximus" (to use a politer term). Besides being a metaphorical pain, it caused a real pain. The constant lifting of this heavy plate gave me a hernia, which eventually led to an operation.

We paid a watchman who patrolled the neighborhood in the evenings, but we didn't trust him to really protect our house, so we got a dog. It was big, savage, and vicious. And as a bonus, it had ticks. One evening we came back from Neusa's parents' to find ticks crawling up the back wall of our bedroom. You don't know what disgusting is until you find a wall in your house teeming with bloated ticks. That was the last straw. We decided to sell the house.

But we made two stupid, costly mistakes: we sold it privately by advertising in the newspaper (of course nowadays nobody advertises in the newspaper, and, sadly, the way things are going, sometime in the future my youngest grandchildren might even wonder what a newspaper is) instead of using a realtor. The second mistake was not asking anyone for advice. Why I never asked anyone for advice before selling I don't know. (Hello, Freud!) The result was that we sold our house for less than it was actually worth.

# CHAPTER 72

# SÃO JOSÉ DO RIO NEGRO

**Sometime around the end of 1982, we sold** our house in Conjunto Manauense and bought an apartment in São José do Rio Negro, a condo complex located on Paraíba Street. Our apartment was spacious, came with light fixtures (remember, our previous apartment didn't), didn't require me to get a workout lifting a heavy metal plate, was safe (no need for a guard dog), and didn't come with ticks climbing up the walls.

Before we moved in, something shocking happened. Well, it wasn't literally shocking, but that was only by a piece of good luck. The final touches were being put on the interior (painting, putting in light fixtures, etc.). We went to the apartment to see how things were coming along. While Neusa and I were looking at the living room, Sérgio, who was four, wandered into one of the bedrooms. On the floor there was an electrical wire and a pair of pliers.

Can you see what's coming? Sérgio picked up the pliers and cut the wire. There was a popping noise—not an explosion, but a loud pop—and all the lights in our apartment went out. Luckily the pliers were insulated, so Sérgio wasn't hurt, just shocked (in the sense of "startled"). We ran into the bedroom and were relieved to find Sérgio OK, just sitting on the floor crying.

It was a nice apartment. No. It was much better than nice. It was fantastic. Just what we were looking for. In a word, it seemed perfect. But we only stayed a few months.

So what caused us to leave our perfect apartment and this after only a few months? I panicked. The monthly mortgage payment was more than my budget comfortably allowed. I had to give extra classes in the evening to make ends meet. So we rented our apartment (which we eventually sold), moved into a rented house (paying less), and looked for something closer to Neusa's parents, where we had always wanted to live (coming home from work and then driving to her parents' was stressful).

After a few months, we found a house for sale not far from Neusa's parents. The house was advertised by a lawyer named Jorge Levy. He required a sum of money to hold the house for us as a guarantee that we were acting in good faith. I didn't have the upfront money he demanded, but I did have a phone line (at that time, you had to buy the phone line, and it was quite expensive). So I offered our phone line, which he accepted.

I soon discovered that *he* wasn't acting in good faith. He wasn't the owner of the house and thus couldn't sell it (it actually belonged to his mother, who lived in Rio de Janeiro; I don't think she even knew her son was selling the house). I tried to get out of the deal and get my phone back but was unsuccessful and lost my phone line.

But this story had a happy ending. (Coincidentally, on the air at 7 p.m. was a soap opera called "Final Feliz"—"happy ending.") We found a house to rent on Silva Ramos, a few blocks from Neusa's parents. Right where we wanted to live.

# CHAPTER 73

# SILVA RAMOS

In September of 1983, we found a house on Silva Ramos that was for rent. It was a two-story house, joined to the houses on either side. On one side there was a dental clinic and on the other a family, but later the property was sold and became the dermatology clinic of doctor Sinésio Talhari, one of the foremost dermatologists in Manaus (another being my good friend Simão Pecher).

It was a nice house and had a good location. Paula's grade school, middle school, and high school—Colégio Nossa Senhora Auxiliadora—was half a block down the street. There was a supermarket (S. Fuji) and a bakery/bread shop (Lindo Pão) a short walk away. About five houses down the street, there was a corner store where you could buy things like beer and cigarettes (which I didn't), Guaraná (a soft drink made from this Amazonian plant), rice, beans, and toilet paper (not of great quality, but great for that emergency when you've run out of the better-quality toilet paper you bought at the supermarket).

The owner was Horáceo, an older man from Portugal. The Portuguese spoken in Brazil is slightly different from the Portuguese spoken in Portugal, like the difference between British and American English (differences in the meaning of some words and especially differences in pronunciation). The result was that I only understood about seventy percent (or less) of what he said, and unless it was important, I just pretended I had understood.

Half a block away was a video rental store, Total Video, where me and my kids would often spend an hour or so browsing through the videos before finally choosing one or two to take out. In fact, the browsing was as much fun as actually watching the films. Today video stores are a thing of the past, one more thing lost to the internet (for more things lost to the internet, see *100 Things We've Lost to the Internet* by Pamela Paul).

There was a nearby bus route to the university (which permitted me to retire my car). And best of all, it was three blocks from Neusa's parents' house. So, yes, it was a good move.

One day the lawyer who was managing the rental of the house came and told me that the owner wanted to sell the house, and I would be given preference. At that time the banks weren't lending money for people to buy houses (there was a temporary hold). But the president of the Amazonas State Bank (BEA), Manuel Ribeiro, was a former teacher at the ICBEU. He arranged for the bank to lend me the money, and thus we bought the house in March of 1984, a little less than a year before our son David was born. This reminds me of a Brazilian saying, which loosely translated is "better a friend in the right place than money in the bank."

We had a parrot (bought at Sérgio's insistence, but Neusa was also a big animal lover). We named it "Louro," which is actually a word for parrot in Portuguese; and anyways, I wasn't consulted about the name. That would be like getting a dog and naming it "dog." It usually stayed in an outside area off the dining room (an area that later became my study). When it wasn't there, it was upstairs in the front bedroom. It would walk or kind of hop on the bed chasing David, who was three at the time, trying to peck him, leaving him in tears.

Louro didn't have a large vocabulary and used one of the few words it knew to tell me what it thought of me: SQUAWK. When I came home from work, that's how Louro greeted me. Repeating it loudly many times. SQUAWK    SQUAWK    SQUAWK    SQUAWK.

Louro met a sad death. I had just come home from work. Louro began squawking, and then it did something it had never done before: it took off and flew into the area behind the house. Unfortunately, it flew right into the mouth of our guard dog, who didn't know what to do with it but nevertheless wasn't letting go. Neusa ran out and repeatedly hit the dog (if I had tried hitting that dog, Louro and my hand would've exchanged places), trying to get it to release its unexpected dinner guest. To no avail. Louro was buried in Neusa's parents' backyard.

In June of 1992, I was able to pay off the mortgage on the house. This was in large part thanks to my Aunt Mary, who out of the blue sent me a gift of a thousand dollars. Now you'll be surprised that a thousand dollars could make even the slightest difference in paying off the mortgage on a house.

But that was over thirty years ago, and the house was in Brazil, where the price of houses was much lower than in the US. And then there was the exchange rate. In June of that year, the exchange rate was over 3,000 to 1. Yes, three thousand to one! So, Aunt Mary's gift was worth over three million Brazilian Cruzeiros. (I wish my aunt was alive so I could again thank her and tell her how much her gift meant to me and my family.)

Our children grew up in that house, and because it was so close to Neusa's parents' house, they were always in close, almost daily contact with their maternal grandparents, especially their grandmother, who came over to our house every day, rain or shine, sun or snow. (Now that would be something. Manaus only has two seasons: hot and hotter). So they essentially grew up with their maternal grandparents (and aunts, uncles, and cousins). Few are so lucky. I hardly knew my grandparents (especially my paternal grandparents), but I did grow up surrounded by eighteen aunts and uncles and around twenty-five cousins. And what a blessing it was!

# CHAPTER 74

# MARIA BEATRIZ

**June of 2008 was a busy month. We sold our house** on Silva Ramos and bought an apartment in Maria Beatriz, a twelve-story apartment building on Leonardo Malcher, a ten-minute walk from Neusa's parents' house. It was a complicated and stressful operation. The person buying our house depended on the sale of his house, and the person whose apartment we were buying depended on his closing a deal to buy an apartment on the twelfth floor. It was a chain of buying and selling, each link depending on the link that came before and after. If any of the other deals didn't go through, then mine was also scuttled. Yes, it was stressful, but at least this time we were smart enough to use a realtor to sell our house.

Our apartment was on the eighth floor. There were three bedrooms (one being a master bedroom with a bathroom), another full bathroom, and a half bathroom (toilet and sink) off the living room. Besides the living room/dining room, there was also a small maid's quarters, which we used for storage (our maid didn't live with us). We converted one of the bedrooms into my study. All the rooms/areas were of a good size. Taken together, I would say our apartment was spacious.

Of course, spacious is relative. Our whole apartment would easily fit into Bill Gates's master bedroom. His house has 7 bedrooms (one for each day of the week?), 24 bathrooms (Okay. Only 10 are full bathrooms), 6 kitchens, and 6 fireplaces. There's also a small exercise room (2,500 square feet!), a trampoline room with a 20-foot ceiling (are you kidding me?), a theater, a reception room for 200 guests (so you don't have to sit next to that annoying relative), an outdoor spa, a putting green, two boat docks, and an underground 10-car garage. And a small 60-foot swimming pool (that's as long as one and a half city buses).

Don't get me wrong. I'm not criticizing him for his lavish spending on his house. I greatly admire him. Since 1994, Bill and his ex-wife, Melinda, have donated an incredible forty-five billion dollars to a wide range of humanitarian causes, that include eradicating malaria, just to name one.

Maria Beatriz also came with a swimming pool (slightly smaller than Bill Gates's) located on the rooftop. Even better than the pool (which I never used) was the view. Looking in one direction, you could see the famous Amazon Theater. From another direction, you could see the Rio Negro (the Black River), which a little further down joins the Rio Solimões to form the Amazon River.

Being on the eighth floor had its advantages and its disadvantages. On the positive side, we had a nice view (we couldn't see the river, but there was a nice view of the city). The disadvantage was that if there was a fire in the building, we would be in serious trouble. And after we moved in, I discovered there had been two incidents of fires. Someone's air conditioner had caught fire, but it was immediately put out. This was always a concern for me because most people in the building ran their air conditioners day and night, meaning there was always a possibility of overheating and catching fire.

Then there was the lady who left a pan on the stove and went out. The building maintenance man just happened to be doing some work near her apartment. He saw smoke coming out from under her kitchen door (which opens out to the floor hallway where he was working). He shouted, and nobody answered. He then broke down the door and took the smoldering pan off the stove.

Of course, that was when the lady came back, and boy was she mad. She was mad as a hornet. (It didn't matter to her that her apartment could've caught fire and engulfed the whole building.) She threatened to sue the maintenance man and the building as a legal entity. (I don't think she actually did sue, and I don't know who paid for replacing the door). One thing I do know. Not only was she as mad as a hornet, but she was also as mad as a hatter.

We stayed in Maria Beatriz for just over two years (until 2010), when we sold it and moved to the United States to be closer to our kids.

# CHAPTER 75

# IF YOU ARE BRAZILIAN,...

Here are some cultural observations made by Brazilians posted on the internet (2023). They seem accurate for my time in Brazil (1972–2010).

### IF YOU ARE BRAZILIAN:

- You like Guaraná better than Coke.
- BBQ means steak, sausage, chicken wings, pork, rice, farofa, and beer.
- You eat rice and beans seven days a week.
- You eat pizza with a knife and a fork.
- You buy bread every day freshly baked at a local bakery.
- Your breakfast consists of a glass of warm milk with a little sweetened coffee and a skillet-toasted French bread roll.
- Your entire family goes to grandma's house on Sundays for lunch and a family get-together.
- You have a large extended family of aunts, uncles, and cousins who you see often.
- You live at home with your parents until you get married.

- You expect to take care of your parents when they are elderly.

- You are hooked on the "novelas" (a kind of soap opera).

- You are the loudest person in the room.

- You leave your house spotless when you have people coming over.

- Your ideal woman has small breasts and a big butt.

- You have a sense of rhythm and can dance.

- You have a sense of fashion and are a smart dresser.

- You wear speedos (men's brief, tight swimming trunks) or a tanga (thong, if you are a woman) to the beach.

- You stand closer to people when talking than Americans do.

- You make jokes about the Portuguese people.

- You take soccer seriously.

- You know how to play volleyball and dominoes.

- You know how to party and expect parties to begin after ten and end in the early hours of the morning.

- You take one or more (in the summer) showers a day.

- You greet friends with a kiss on each cheek.

- You dress in white for New Years to bring good luck.

- You think Rio de Janeiro is the most beautiful city in the world.

# PART SEVEN:

# SEATTLE

# (2010-PRESENT)

# CHAPTER 76

# OUR KIDS MOVE TO THE US

**Let me begin by saying we never encouraged our** kids to leave Brazil and move to the States. We would have preferred that they stayed in Brazil, preferably in Manaus. All three have dual citizenship. Having been born in Brazil, they are Brazilian. But soon after their births, I registered them with the American Embassy, which gave them American citizenship. For some reason, it had always been Sergio's dream to live in the US. That was from a very young age, maybe as early as fourteen. As I said, we never encouraged it, nor did we ever even talk about the idea.

But Sergio became intent on going to live in the US. If I were to say that Sergio was persistent, that would be an understatement. When he put something in his head, that was all you would hear from him (morning, noon, and night) until he got what he wanted (and persistent, he still is!).

We always treated all three kids the same, but Sérgio managed to get what he wanted a little (a lot?) more often than his brother or sister. He got what he wanted by wearing us down, tiring us out, and we would give in. That persistence eventually got him to the US.

It was the year 2000. He wanted me to ask my sister, his Aunt Maureen, if he could come and stay a few months. I didn't want to do this because, in this respect, American culture is a little different from Brazilian culture. In Brazil, it's common to send your son or daughter to live for a while with your brother or sister in another city. Thus, a person from Manaus might send her son to live with her sister in Rio de Janeiro while he studies at the Federal University.

So, I was hesitant to ask her. But finally I did ask, but only indirectly. I called her and said, "Sergio would like to come to the States for a month or two. By any chance, do you know any family who might be willing to take him in for a month or two?" She said she would check. A few hours later she called me back and told me that she had consulted with Joel (her husband), and Sérgio could come stay with them for two months.

Thus, in the summer of 2000, Sérgio and I went to Seattle. I stayed for two weeks. Before I returned to Brazil, Sérgio, with the help of his Uncle Joel, got a job bagging groceries at a supermarket. Not long after that, Sérgio rented an apartment with Zé Neto, one of his best friends from Manaus, who came to Seattle to study.

In 2001, Paula moved to the States. She also received a lot of support from Maureen and Joel. She moved in with Sérgio and Zé Neto. The story of her move to the States is different from Sérgio's. Paula never had a desire to leave Brazil. She had graduated from the University of Amazonas with a degree in public relations (graduating first in her class; equivalent to being valedictorian); she had a boyfriend; and she had a good job. But it was her "good" job that eventually led her to leave Brazil.

In 2000, McDonald's opened a franchise in Manaus. Paula was one of fifteen selected (out of 1,500 applicants) to open and manage the new McDonald's. Being a manager at the first McDonald's in Manaus was a prestigious job. Paula's hours were long, and the work was demanding. But that wasn't what led her to leave McDonald's and move to the States.

In 2000, there was an election, and in Brazil voting is obligatory. There are consequences if you fail to vote (for example, you can't renew your passport). It was getting towards the end of the day, and Paula needed to leave her post at McDonald's and go to her voting station. The owner of the franchise made her stay until it was almost too late for her to get to her voting station, and she arrived home in tears.

That was the second bad work experience. Before McDonald's, she was the marketing manager for a company that produces and sells natural Amazonian health, cosmetic, and beauty supplies. When she brought it to the management's attention that her salary was inconsistent with her university degree and training, the CEO said, "Honey, do you see that door over there? Well, on the other side, there are dozens who would just love to have your job." Two bad work experiences and not a lot of future prospects if she were to change jobs.

Her boyfriend suggested that she should join Sérgio in the States and that he would soon follow. It didn't work out for him to go; they broke up, and six months later Paula met Thomas. In July of 2003, Paula and Thomas got married. Of course, me, Neusa, and David came to Seattle for the wedding. David had planned to stay in the States and live with Sérgio, but at the last minute he changed his mind and returned to Manaus with me and Neusa. Then six months later, he decided he wanted to go and be with his brother and sister. So, in December of 2003, David left Manaus and went to live with Sérgio.

# CHAPTER 77

# WE FOLLOW OUR KIDS

**One by one, our kids moved to Seattle, where** my sister was living. Sergio went first in 2000, Paula went in 2001, and David in 2003. Neusa's mother died in 2007. Then, two years later, in December of 2009, Neusa's father died.

After the passing of Neusa's parents, we began the process of getting Neusa an immigration visa. You would think that since she was married to an American it would be easy, especially considering we had been married for over thirty-six years. The length of our marriage is important because it proves it wasn't a sham marriage, a marriage just so she could get a Green Card.

I often kidded Neusa, saying she married me just to get a Green Card. She never thought it was funny! And she would then immediately remind me that the boyfriend she broke up with to marry me was rich and had a mansion in Petropolis, one of the most beautiful cities in Brazil.

So, in January of 2010, we began the Green Card process. The first step was to fill out an application and take it to an American consulate (the application had to be submitted *in person*). Since Neusa had a dear aunt (Tia Rosália) in Rio, we decided to do it there (a four-hour flight from Manaus).

The whole process was stressful. The application asked for a staggering amount of information and documents, all of which had to be assembled in a precise and specific order (I have a suspicion that one of the requirements for being a consul is having worked at McDonald's, which has a very specific way of performing every task). Just one example: I had to list every single trip we had ever made to the US, including when, where, and how long we had stayed. There had been many trips, so you can imagine how hard it was to get that right.

And to make things worse, communication with the consulate wasn't easy. Basically, any doubts had to be clarified via email, since the immigration office would only take calls on Fridays between nine and noon.

So we went to Rio, handed in the application, visited Neusa's aunt, and five days later returned to Manaus. While this was going on, I was being investigated (by the FBI?) to be sure I wasn't a criminal or a terrorist. I should've given my friend Ricardo Bianco as a character reference. He would've told them I was an honest, hard-working teacher and that on the side I also worked for the US government as a CIA agent. Bianco always kidded me, saying he thought my being a teacher was just a cover for my real profession as a spy.

The next step was a return to Rio for Neusa to have a physical exam, which had to be at an approved clinic. We returned to Manaus and then a few weeks later went back to Rio for Neusa's interview with the consul.

Neusa went into the interview, and then I was called in. I couldn't imagine there would be a problem, but there was. I had to prove that I could financially support Neusa. The consul said he couldn't accept the value I had put for the sale of our condo because it was in the process of being sold, and thus he would need the final sale document (which should've been irrelevant since my salary itself was above the amount required).

So back to Manaus to conclude the sale of our condo, which occurred shortly after we returned from Rio. I had the option of sending the document of the sale via registered express mail, but I opted to take it personally. So once again I flew to Rio.

Since we had sold our condo, we had to turn it over to the new owners. We went to Hotel do Largo, a small, clean hotel near the famous Amazon Theater, owned by my friend Pedro Mendonça. The perfect place to spend our last days in Manaus.

There was still a certain amount of stress before we actually left Manaus. We had made our flight arrangements and were staying in a hotel, but we couldn't leave the country without the immigration document. So, every day I had to go back to our condo building and check if the document had arrived, always worrying it wouldn't arrive in time for us to take the flight we had booked.

We finally left Manaus in July of 2010. We flew to Miami, where Neusa had an immigration interview, which went fine. Of course, we had more suitcases than permitted. I'll only comment on one of the additional suitcases. This suitcase had only one item: a very large doll that many moons ago had belonged to …. Paula (you didn't think it belonged to me, did you?). Neusa brought this doll for our granddaughters, Isabella and Giovanna. I didn't want to bring the doll (such an unsentimental father/grandfather!). So, we did the democratic thing. We took a vote. I voted to leave the doll, and Neusa voted to take the doll. Since my vote didn't count, we brought the doll.

# CHAPTER 78

# LOSING NEUSA

**We moved from Manaus to Seattle in July of** 2010. We spent about two weeks living at Paula's house while we located and rented an apartment. We found a nice apartment called King Arthur's Court. It was spacious: a master bedroom with a bathroom and a walk-in closet, a second bedroom, a second full bathroom, a combination living room/dining room, and a small kitchen. And best of all, it was only a ten-minute walk to Paula's house.

There were two important things I did right away. The first was to get a health plan. The second was to buy a cemetery plot. Little did I know that that decision would turn out to be so important: you don't want to have to make funeral arrangements when you have just lost someone.

A little before Christmas of 2010, Neusa began to experience nausea. Her primary care doctor felt it was acid reflux, but as the condition persisted, Neusa was scheduled to have an endoscopy at the end of January. In the morning of January 23, 2011, around 7 a.m., Neusa went into the bathroom, and then I heard a thud. Neusa had passed out. I got her up and back in bed and called my kids, who came and took us to the emergency room at Virgina Mason Hospital. She was in the hospital from January 23rd to February 18th. It was gall bladder cancer, and sadly it was not treatable.

When Neusa took ill, the boys broke the lease on their apartment and moved into our building, on the same floor, just down the hall. Every morning before leaving for work, Sérgio would come over to have breakfast with us. David wouldn't come for breakfast as he had to leave the house at 6 a.m. but would call his mother every day at noon. Paula would come over every day around nine, help Neusa make lunch (Neusa cooked until near the end of her illness), and stay for lunch with us.

The last month, Neusa was weak and in constant discomfort and pain. Luckily, the health plan had provisions for a nurse to come every day to administer medicine. The boys took time off from their work to be able to give full-time support to their mother. In fact, they moved in with us, sleeping in our second bedroom.

On Thursday, October 6th, the nurse asked if it wouldn't be better for Neusa to go to a facility that provides comfort care for the terminally ill in their last days. We all agreed that this was the best choice as we could no longer manage to make her comfortable at home. She was taken by ambulance to the Evergreen Hospice. There she was in a comfortable room with round-the-clock nursing care. The room was big enough to accommodate me and my three kids, and thus we all spent the last days and nights together with Neusa.

By the end of that evening, all verbal communication from her had ceased. By Friday, her lips would move, but no sound would come out, and her eyes were always closed. However, on Saturday, somehow she was able to muster her forces and extend her hand to Isabella, our six-year-old granddaughter.

Sunday, October 9th, in the early morning (2 a.m.), she passed away. We were in the room, but asleep. The nurse woke us up and told us that Neusa had passed. We stayed in the room with Neusa for about half an hour and then went home, Paula to her house and me and the boys to my apartment. When we got back to my apartment, nobody said a word. Sergio went into the second bedroom, and David, without speaking, climbed in bed with me. In addition to their own personal pain, my kids were worried about me.

There are two inexplicable stories related to Neusa's illness and passing. At my granddaughter's school, a Catholic school, there was a sale of small Christmas items that the kids could buy to give to members of their family. Isabella bought a small medallion with the picture of a saint who is supposed to work miracles. She gave it to Neusa and said, "This is my Christmas present for you. You are going to need it." How could Isabella (age five) have had any idea that her grandmother was going to need the help of that saint, especially since this was a month before Neusa became ill?

My two granddaughters visited Neusa at the hospice (at that time Neusa was no longer able to communicate). Both were very young (ages three and six) and, of course, couldn't understand what was happening. The hospice gave each of them a small stuffed animal. A few months after Neusa died, Giovanna lost her stuffed animal. One day, Paula woke up and said to Thomas, "I want to go to the Goodwill store in Edmonds" (a city about twenty minutes from Paula's house).

Paula never shopped at Goodwill or any other thrift store. Never. (Out of the question then, but not today.) So this was a strange request. And what's even stranger, she wanted to go to a specific store, not the store located near her house. At that store, there was a barrel full of stuffed animals. Among the many stuffed animals, Paula found the exact stuffed animal that the hospice had given to Giovanna.

I don't believe in an afterlife. I think when it's over, it's over. Finished. Done. Cést fini. I tend to agree with British physicist Stephen Hawking (1942–2018), who said that heaven, or afterlife, is "a fairy tale for people afraid of the dark."

However, this incident gives me pause, makes me wonder if somehow Neusa was communicating with Paula from the hereafter. You never know. I mean, Steve Jobs's last words were "Oh wow. Oh wow. Oh wow."

Afterlife or not, the two saddest words in English are "forever" and "nevermore."

# CHAPTER 79

# AFTER NEUSA

**After Neusa died, I continued living in the King** Arthur's Court apartment. During the mornings and early afternoons, I would (and still do) spend my time working on various teaching-related projects. Although I'm retired, I still enjoy reading about teaching English as a foreign language and producing teaching materials. Because I'm busy with my projects and am always with my kids and grandkids, I never have time to feel lonely, depressed, or sorry for myself.

In June of 2012, I went on a cruise to Alaska with Sérgio and David. I loved every minute of it except for the two hours they spent on a helicopter tour that landed on top of a glacier. I did NOT enjoy watching them go up in what seemed like a not-so-safe helicopter. (I was almost sixty-five at the time, and my mind was fine, meaning I was neither senile nor crazy to the point that I would accompany them on that adventure.)

Sérgio was always a daring, audacious thrill-seeker. When he was seventeen, he did his first skydive. I still remember looking up and seeing what at first appeared to be a small coin in the sky and realizing that it was my son. Some years later, he went hang-gliding from a height of 1,700 feet (as high as a 170-story building) from "Pedra Bonita" in Rio de Janeiro.

King Arthur's office is located right off the elevator. When

I would go out, I would often first stop in the office and have a short chat with the manager, Kalina Lisica. One day (in February of 2014), when I stopped in the office, she said, "One minute, there's a new resident in the building. I think you would like to meet her. She's from Brazil." A few minutes later, in walked Socorro (Maria do Socorro Pires Cruz), who was in Seattle doing post-doctorate work. We immediately began speaking Portuguese, and it felt like we were two old friends who hadn't seen each other for a long time.

This reminds me of another time, years earlier, when I spoke Portuguese to two Brazilians and got a very different response. It was around 1975. Neusa and I were in an elevator, somewhere in Los Angeles, and we heard two girls (probably in their twenties) speaking Portuguese. I turned to them and said, "São brasileiras?" (Are you Brazilian?) to which one of them replied, "Não. Somos Paulistas" ("Paulista" is someone from the state of São Paulo). That's like someone asking, "Are you American?" and receiving the reply, "No, I'm Texan."

In the summer of 2014, Ringo Starr was performing at a winery in Seattle. I went with Socorro, her friend Alessandra (who was visiting), and my son David. Everyone was seated on the grass. As Ringo and his band performed, many "older" attendees (dressed like they were still living in the sixties) got up and began to dance. As I looked at those "displaced hippies" dancing, I thought, "My God. I've come to a geriatrics convention!" (Maybe I should've asked Socorro if she had a mirror.)

In 2014, we went to a séance in the hopes of communicating with Neusa. I know this sounds (and is) irrational, but when the opportunity presented itself, we decided we had nothing to lose. Sergio was working at Harborview Hospital as a radiology technician. A patient he was performing an exam on hinted that he was a medium and said he could get Sérgio in contact with his deceased mother.

So, a few days later, we (me, Paula, David, and Sérgio) went to this guy's house. After some time, the guy said that the spirit of Neusa was in the room, and we could receive her thoughts through him. But when he said that Neusa wanted to communicate to us that she didn't approve of David's girlfriend (Mirella), I knew he was a charlatan because I knew for sure that Neusa would approve of Mirella and would gladly welcome her into the family.

In 2015, I received a shock. I never took a course in creative writing, but I know a sentence like that is a good way to begin because it creates suspense. My pension is in Brazilian currency and is deposited into my account in Brazil every month. I then transfer it, at the exchange rate of the day, to my account in Seattle. My shock came when I logged on to my account in Brazil and saw that the dollar had shot up, which meant I needed many more Brazilian Reais for every American dollar.

It soon became apparent I would have to move from my apartment. I contemplated moving back to Brazil (where my pension would be fine). Then Paula and Thomas suggested I could live with them. They had a very spacious room (a family room) that was not being used. So that's how in 2015 I came to live with Paula and her family.

# PART EIGHT:

# A FEW MORE STORIES

# CHAPTER 80

# A TALE OF TWO CAROLS

**It was the best of times; it was the worst of times.** Isn't that a great way to begin? Doesn't it make you want to read more? The problem is those words aren't mine. I borrowed (OK, stole) them from British author Charles Dickens (1812–1870). That's how he began his famous novel *A Tale of Two Cities,* and as you can see, I also kind of plagiarized his title.

The first Carol I'm going to talk about was, unfortunately, my first girlfriend. I say "unfortunately" because she should've been my second girlfriend, not my first, but my "almost" first girlfriend didn't become a girlfriend, so Carol became my first girlfriend (confusing, isn't it?). So my story actually begins BC (before Carol, and not "before Christ," but it does seem so long ago).

It was spring semester of 1967; I was nineteen and in my last year at Los Angeles Valley College. My "almost" first girlfriend, Carmen, was a pretty, olive-skinned "Chicana," that is, a girl of Mexican descent (a male would be a "Chicano"). The word "Chicano" had (and still has) positive connotations: recognition and appreciation of Mexican culture (which is so much a part of California's culture).

I like the name Carmen. It brings to mind my niece Carmem (daughter of Neusa's brother João), who looks so much like Neusa that looking at her, you see an earlier Neusa. It also brings to mind Carmen Miranda (1909–1955), the Portuguese-born Brazilian singer, dancer, and actress (nicknamed "The Brazilian Bombshell"), who was known for her signature fruit hat. In the 1940s, Carmen Miranda brought attention to Brazilian music and culture.

There was going to be a party at a friend's house. I invited Carmen (sadly, not Carmen Miranda), and that party became our first and only date. I made a comment about a ring she was wearing. I was naïve. I just thought it was a pretty ring, nothing else. It was then that she told me that it was an engagement ring, that she was engaged to be married, but had some reservations (a case of cold feet). We continued to talk on campus but never again went out on a date.

In the fall of 1967, not long before my 20th birthday, I began my studies at UCLA. I was living in Rieber Hall, a student dorm. I was on the third floor, rooming with my friend Stan Levinson. At one end of the floor, there was a room that could be used as a quiet place to study or for a social event. Someone invited the girls who lived on the same floor as ours in the women's wing to come to a party in that room. There were chips and soft drinks (nothing alcoholic). Someone brought a stereo and lots of LPs.

That's where I met Carol. I guess you could say those dorm parties were the Match.com of the 1960s. We started dating. We dated from September of 1967 until spring of 1968. Here's how it ended. It was a Sunday afternoon. The dorm had certain rules on when you could invite someone from the opposite sex up to your room. The permitted times were Saturday evening and Sunday afternoon.

Each room had a phone. You dialed (no touch phone yet) the room number you wanted to be connected to. I called Carol's room. To my surprise, Big Richard answered the phone. The guy who answered the phone was neither tall nor brawny nor burly. In fact, his name wasn't even Richard. In Brazil, "Big Richard" (Ricardão) is an expression signifying a man who is "the other" in a relationship. So, we broke up. It wasn't a sad ending. It just ended, and I don't think she even had a relationship with "Big Richard."

The second Carol. It was 1970. I was twenty-two, and I worked as a programs assistant at UCLA's International Student Center. Carol worked in the International Student Affairs Office. I asked her out for New Year's Eve (end of 1970). First we went out to dinner in Westwood Village, which at that time catered to university students. (Today everything in Westwood Village is "high end.")

Now, you have to remember, I was a student at that time. When we got to the restaurant and I saw the prices, I realized I didn't have enough money to pay for both of our dinners! It was a problem, and I was too embarrassed to tell her the truth. My solution was to order only a bowl of soup for my dinner. I don't remember what she ordered. Afterwards, we watched the New Year come in. For some reason, I didn't ask her out again. In fact, I don't remember talking to her after that (but I must have). Once again, Hello Freud!

# CHAPTER 81

# DISASTROUS DATES

**First dates can be good, fun, enjoyable, and lead to** further dates and a relationship. They can also be something less than what was hoped for. When I was young, like everyone else, I had my share of both good and not-so-good dates. The dates I'm going to talk about weren't actually disasters; they were just "not so good."

My first "disastrous" date was a blind date. I was eighteen and a student at Los Angeles Valley College. My friends Bill Gray and Elaine Harris suggested that we go on a double date, and since I didn't have a girlfriend, they fixed me up with Elaine's neighbor, Marilyn.

I had never met her, but the name was auspicious since it brought to mind Marilyn Monroe, an actress who was one of the most popular sex symbols of the 1950s and early 1960s, certainly one of the most famous of all times.

Marilyn Monroe (1926–1962) was famous for playing comedic "dumb blond" characters in films like *Gentlemen Prefer Blondes* (1953); *How to Marry a Millionaire* (1953); and *Some Like It Hot* (1959), a film about two musicians who disguise themselves by dressing as women to escape from mafia gangsters who they had witnessed committing a crime.

When she sang "Happy Birthday, Mr. President" at

President John F. Kennedy's 45th birthday celebration, she "stole the show" with her sultry performance and her provocative costume (a beige, skintight dress covered in rhinestones, which made her appear nude).

On August 4, 1962, Marylin was found dead in her Los Angeles mansion. Although it was ruled a suicide, there were speculations that she had been murdered to cover up supposed affairs with both President Kennedy and his brother, Attorney General Robert Kennedy. (Apparently the two brothers were close and believed in the adage "Caring is Sharing.")

That was a long aside to my disastrous date, which will only take a sentence or two. Bill and Elaine were in the front seat, and me and Marilyn were in the back seat. I put my arm over her shoulder, and she turned to me and said, "Did you do that on purpose?" That's the only thing I remember about that first and last date. No, I don't remember what I said.

The next one was with a girl from my English class at Valley College, around 1966. I again double-dated with Bill and Elaine. We went to a party at a friend's house, and at some point in the evening my date informed me that she had found someone else to spend the party with and that that person would be taking her home.

In retrospect, I should've sued her. Suing is as American as apple pie, cowboys, baseball, hot dogs, Thanksgiving, and Black Friday shopping. Americans sue for anything and everything. Here are two examples. The first was for a situation somewhat similar to mine. In 1978, Tom Horsley, a 41-year-old accountant, was upset when his date for the evening failed to show up, so he sued her for "breach of oral contract," asking for $38 in compensation for time lost and travel expenses. The judge ruled against him. Then there's the man from Pennsylvania who sued the Devil. He claimed that Satan had placed obstacles in his life that had caused his downfall. The court dismissed the suit, saying, "The defendant (Satan) didn't reside in the state."

My last "disastrous date" was with a magician. It was my senior year at UCLA, spring quarter of 1969. Near the campus there was a pizza parlor (the Pizza Palace) where you could take a date or go there alone hoping to meet someone. There was sawdust on the floor and live music by a singer named Skip, who performed Beatles songs like *Hey Jude, Revolution,* and *Back in the U.S.S.R.* When he wasn't singing, *Road Runner* cartoons were projected on a screen on the wall.

On this particular evening, I met a girl there. We had a pizza and a couple of beers and went to Santa Monica Beach to watch the waves. When we got to the beach, the beer began to take effect, and I went to a nearby public restroom to "take the water from my knee," which is a Brazilian expression meaning to "pee."

When I got back, she was gone. I looked in all directions, but she was gone. She had disappeared. Like magic. (I told you she was a magician.) I waited for about an hour, and then I left. If this had been the army, she would've been considered AWOL (absent without leave) or, in another army expression, MIA (missing in action). Another "disastrous" date. I had others, but none come to mind.

CHAPTER 82

# MY BIRTHDAYS

I don't remember many of my (so far) seventy-six birthdays (maybe Freud can explain this), but before sharing two that I do remember, let's look at how birthdays are celebrated around the world.

In Brazil, the birthday celebration is often a big party in a rented hall. There's always an elaborate table filled with sweets, especially fudge balls (known as "brigadeiros"). A birthday party without 'brigadeiros' would be like Thanksgiving without a turkey. In India, on their birthdays, children wear colorful clothing to school and pass out chocolates to the entire class. But what I like most is that they also kneel and touch their parents' feet as a sign of respect. If only I had known about this custom when my kids were young!

In Argentina, the birthday child receives a tug on the ear for each year they have been alive. In Hungary, it's traditional to continuously pull the ears of the birthday person while reciting a poem wishing them a life as long as their ears will be when they touch the floor.

In the United States, children receive a soft spank on their bottom for each year and then another for good luck. At least that was common when I was a child. There's a cake with candles, one for each year. The birthday person makes a wish and tries to blow out all the candles with one breath. If they succeed, then the wish will come true. Which reminds me of what the great British-American comic and entertainer Bob Hope (1903–2003) once said: "You know you're getting old when the candles cost more than the cake."

My first birthday memory was when I turned fifteen. I don't remember having a party, but maybe I did. That year (1962), one of my favorite classes was biology, in which we dissected frogs. Just before my birthday, I went to my biology teacher and asked if I could have a frog to dissect at home, to which he consented. So that's how I spent my fifteenth birthday, dissecting a frog.

Which reminds me of the time a lonely frog consulted a fortune-teller who said, "You are going to meet a beautiful young girl, and she will want to know everything about you." "That's great!" said the excited frog. "When will I meet her?" "Next semester," replied the psychic, "in her biology class."

Jump ahead five years. It's 1967. I live on campus at Rieber Hall, room with my friend Stan Levinson, and have a girlfriend, Carol (the "Big Richard" Carol). One day, about three weeks before my birthday (twenty years), Stan asked me what I was planning to do for my birthday. I told him I planned to go to Carol's and spend it with her. Stan replied, "That's a good idea." Then two days later he again asked what I was going to do for my birthday, and I again told him I was going to go to Carol's. Once again, he said, "That's a good idea." Then a few days later, a third time, he again asked me what I was going to do for my birthday.

That, of course, gave it away. I was then sure of what I had already suspected: the group of dorm friends I always had dinner with were planning a surprise party for my birthday at Carol's house. Come my birthday, I needed my father to drive me to Carol's house because he needed the family car that evening. Dad was taking his time getting ready to take me, so I said something like, "Dad, can you hurry? They're planning a surprise party for me, and I don't want to be late." I got a lot of fun gag gifts. There's one I remember in particular, actually the only one. At the time I had a mustache and a kind of goatee, except it wasn't pointed. So someone gave me a small jar of Nair, a well-known depilatory.

Strangely, those are the only birthdays of which I have any memories. Today (2024), my birthday is celebrated with a small family get-together. There's a cake but no candles (that many wouldn't fit on the cake; not even on two cakes), and *Happy Birthday* is sung twice, first in English and then in Portuguese. So nice to have a Brazilian-American family: I get two renditions of *Happy Birthday* and two Father's Day celebrations (in Brazil it's in August).

# CHAPTER 83

# FREUD CAN EXPLAIN

**Maybe Freud can explain my aversion to driving;** explain why I gave up driving more than thirty years ago. To begin with, I wasn't a typical teenage boy. I had no interest in cars and no interest in driving. For me, a car was always just a pragmatic necessity, something that could carry me from one place to another. But for many others, cars have a special attraction and play more than just a pragmatic role in their lives.

My son-in-law, Thomas, can tell you the make and model of any car that passes by. He can tell you the year the car was first launched, the horsepower, the number of pistons, and the average gas mileage, among many other things of which I have absolutely no knowledge, understanding, or interest in knowing about.

Me? The only car I can identify is the old Volkswagen Beetle. I have never failed in my attempts to identify that car. Every time I've seen a VW Beetle, I've been able to identify it and assure everyone that it was indeed a Beetle and not a Rolls Royce or a Lamborghini.

I bought my first car in 1968. The car was a 1959 Ford. Actually, the car was only half mine since I bought it together with my brother. I don't remember how long we had the car, but one day he came up to me and told me that he was selling his half of the car. Either I gave him the money for his half, or we sold the car together, or he would sell his half to someone else. So we sold the car.

It was in this car that occurred an incident that left a psychological mark. It occurred with my girlfriend, Donna (the one I lost to a pineapple in Hawaii). The incident was traffic-related. What kind of a guy do you think I am?

It was sometime in 1968. We were on our way to a hypnotist show. Donna said, "Aren't you going to stop?" (no reaction from me). "You had better STOP!!!" (spoken with an urgency that got my attention and brought my mind back from wherever it was to the current situation.) There was a car stopped not too far ahead, and a guy was changing a tire. I hate to think of what would've happened if my girlfriend hadn't alerted me. That incident really had a psychological effect on me (Hello, Freud).

My first car in Brazil was a Ford Corcel. The year was 1981. There was only one small problem. I had never driven a stick shift; my car in the United States had an automatic transmission. Now, for most people that wouldn't be a problem, but in my case it was because I'm not what you would call "coordinated." Which reminds me of what President Lyndon Johnson once said about Gerald Ford (1913–2006), later President Ford: "He can't fart and chew gum at the same time," which the media changed to "can't walk." That would've been an apt description of my motor coordination then and now.

So I took driving lessons. During one of the lessons, on a road leading to a suburb, my friend Eduardo Lleras passed my car (a driving school car) and honked. I didn't respond. A few days later we ran into each other, and he asked me why I hadn't waved to him. I told him I hadn't seen him, nor had I heard the honk. I had all I could do to concentrate on where my hands and feet were. It's a good thing I wasn't also chewing gum.

Around 1993, I had a red Fiat. One evening I went with the family to the mall. Sérgio was fourteen, Paula sixteen, and David eight. Coming out of the mall, the car stalled. Unfortunately, the place where it chose to stall was in a major exit, and I was blocking a long line of cars, which resulted in clamorous honking from the cars behind me. I used every curse word I knew in English and then some. The swearing didn't get the car started. Well, maybe it helped because the car decided to work again.

On the way home, along a busy road, the car once again "gave up the ghost." Sérgio got out to push the car, and I remained inside to steer. Then two things happened, one good and one scary. First the scary. A bus nearly hit Sérgio. It was really a close call. The good thing is that the car once again decided to work, and we made it home. That was the last straw. I sold the car, and we depended on taxis, which actually worked out well, as Manaus had many reliable taxi companies, and taxis weren't expensive.

And there were other benefits. I didn't have to worry about putting gas in the car, changing the oil, checking the tire pressure, fixing a flat tire, taking the car to a mechanic for repairs, finding a parking space, dealing with rude, impatient, and (sometimes) belligerent drivers, and (especially) paying attention while driving (in the taxi, I could think about my lesson plans for the day or what Neusa was making for dinner).

Sometime around 1994, one of the cab companies sent me a driver named "Bueno." He was Brazilian but had a name that was a common Spanish word that means "good." I immediately saw that he was indeed a "good man." I would always call Bueno directly when I needed a taxi. It wasn't long before we worked out a system. For each ride, he would write down the date, where I went, and the amount I owed. At the end of the month, he would tally up the rides, and I would make a payment. It was a good system for both of us: I didn't have to worry about having cash available, and he received a fairly large one-time payment instead of small amounts dripping in.

# FINIS AND A LITTLE BOOMER WISDOM

Thus ends my story. FINIS (which is Latin for "the end"). C'est fini (see, more proof that I did learn some French). That sounds kind of pessimistic. Like I'm about to "Kick the bucket"; "Buy the farm" (I never wanted to be a farmer anyway); "Cash in my chips" (I always lost at poker); "Push up daisies" (that will be hard to do since I will be cremated—cheaper than buying a coffin); and, finally, "Meet my Maker." Meeting my maker reminds me of two things: Churchill (1874–1965) famously said, "I am prepared to meet my Maker. Whether my Maker is prepared for the ordeal of meeting me is another matter." The second thing is, whenever I'm introduced to my kids' friends, I always say, "I'm their maker." At any rate, I'm still alive and kicking and expect my story to continue for a number of years.

I hope you have enjoyed my stories as much as I have enjoyed remembering (and researching) them and putting them down in words.

I always joke with my kids, saying their birthday present will be an hour of fatherly advice (but I already told you that). So, I thought I would end with some pieces of advice taken from *The Complete Life's Little Instruction Book* by H. Jackson Brown and my dear Uncle Harold. First from Jackson Brown (with a few of my own):

- Live within your means and Save, Save, Save.

- Have a monthly "date night."

- From time to time, do something romantic and unexpected for your spouse.

- Keep a tight rein on your temper.

- Don't speed, tailgate, or become "enraged."

- Avoid oncoming traffic: drive in the slower right-hand lane.

- Don't be so concerned with your rights that you forget your manners.

- Remember that *how* you say something is as important as *what* you say.

- Admit your mistakes.

- Don't be afraid to say, "I'm sorry. Please forgive me."

- Never underestimate the power of a kind word or deed.

- Don't carry a grudge.

- Give people the benefit of the doubt.

- Be willing to forgive and forget.

- Don't gossip or badmouth people.

- Patronize local merchants, even if it costs a bit more.

- Check for toilet paper before sitting down.

- Read more books; spend less time on your phone.

- Never drive while holding a cup of hot coffee between your knees.

- Life is short. Take time to smell the roses.

- Don't expect life to be fair.

- Don't sweat the small stuff (and most of what irritates us is "small stuff").

- Buy a cemetery plot. I already reserved a space in my son Sérgio's backyard. I wouldn't want to miss his barbecues.

- Put all your important information (bank, credit cards, legal documents, passwords, logins, etc.) in a folder to which a designated person (now) has access.

- Treat others as you would like them to treat you.

- And finally, Never kick a cow patty on a hot day.

I will end with some words of wisdom from my dear uncle Harold, taken and slightly shortened from his book, *The Life of Lucky Pierre.*

"I have been asked as to what has been my philosophy, my aphorism on my life. I believe in family loyalty and family support; in whatever form it takes. I never have felt that marriage was a "50-50" proposition, but that to have a successful marriage you have to go much more. Life is too short to waste time in resentment and anger, make each day count and rejoice in your blessings. Don't "sweat" the petty irritations. Major problems will come to all of us. Change those that you can and accept those that cannot be changed.

The inability to forgive and forget personal slights and offenses is destructive, and I pride myself on not having the nature to harbor long term ill feelings toward anyone. A sense of humor has helped me throughout my adult years. I see the cup as half full, not as half empty." (Harold Chevlen, 1921–2021).

# ACKNOWLEDGMENTS

I would like to acknowledge and thank those who provided technical support and/or encouragement.

This memoir began as a few Facebook posts about how I wound up going to Brazil. There was no intention of writing a memoir. But the many positive comments and suggestions that I should turn my posts into a memoir resulted in my doing so. There are too many of you to name (over seventy), but you know who you are, and it's thanks to your encouragement that this memoir was written.

However, there are three individuals who deserve a special thanks for their encouragement. As I was writing, I would share my stories with my (*unbiased*) sister, Maureen Shallit, who always responded with gushing enthusiastic praise (it was like having all seventy of my Facebook commentators rolled into one rousing cheerleader).

Two friends from Brazil, Dulce-Alencar Lake and Tânia Menezes, were especially important. They interacted with almost every one of my eighty Facebook stories. When my motivation waned, their comments always lifted my spirits and gave me the will to continue writing.

Without the input from my cousins Eric Chevlen, Jim Axelrad, and Jay Stern, the stories of my grandparents couldn't have been written. Eric provided the information on our maternal grandparents (and hopefully won't sue me for plagiarism), and Jim and Jay (second cousins) provided information on my paternal grandparents.

Ruth Alencar Peixoto and Lenise Barbosa gave me feedback on my stories about Manaus; Steve Solomon, Jimmy Witt, Chuck Rumble, and Michael Broida, about Youngstown; and Elaine Steaffens and Gerry Huybregts, about Los Angeles Valley College.

FedEx at the Seattle Lake City store provided exceptionally good service for the bindings of the many "in progress" versions. That store closed, and I then received the same level of excellent service from Mohammed Azmath at Professional Copy/Print (UW district).

The interior was typeset by Kerry Ellis. Rafael Andres produced the cover (using a drawing my granddaughter Isabella did of me when she was eight years old, calling me Mr. Worry). Working with them was an enormous pleasure, and if you're writing a book, I highly recommend using their services. They can be reached at Reedsy.com.

My children (Paula, Sérgio, and David); my son-in-law (Thomas); my daughters-in-law (Angela and Mirella); my granddaughters (Isabella and Giovanna); and my two twin 18-month-old grandsons (Leon and Rafael) are one of the reasons I decided to write this memoir: in large part it's for them.

Finally, my greatest thanks and appreciation go to my wife, Neusa Maria, who sadly is not here to share with me the completion of this project. But her presence is there on every page.

www.ingramcontent.com/pod-product-compliance
Lightning Source LLC
Chambersburg PA
CBHW071714120626
46550CB00001B/230